Boy Scouts Handbook

(The First Edition),

1911

Boy Scouts of America

Published by Dead Authors Society.

Printed and manufactured in the United States of America

CONTENTS

	PAGE
PREFACE	ix
INTRODUCTION	xi
Introduction to the Early Editions	1
The American Flag	5

PART I—ORGANIZATION
(Adapted from B. P.)

Officers, etc.	8
Members	10
Tests	11
Badges and Medals	13
Badges of Merit	14
Medals	19
Uniforms	23
War Songs	25
Crests, Totems, or Patrol Signs	26
Scout Law	31
Summary of Instruction	34

PART II—SIGNS AND SIGNALLING

Morse Code	56
Rememberable Morse	57
Wig-wag or Myer Code	58
Rememberable Myer	59
Semaphore	60
Indian Signs and Blazes	61
The Watch as a Compass	64
Old Sayings and Weather Signs	64
Outdoor Proverbs	66
Measuring Distances	67

PART III—CAMPING

Camping Trips	71
Outfit for Six	72
Tents	74
Teepees	75
Camp-grounds	75
Beds	76
Lights	77

CONTENTS

		PAGE
Water	. . . .	77
Mosquitoes, Black Flies, etc.	. . . .	77
Camp Routine	. . . .	78
Camp-fires	. . . .	79
Use of Firearms	. . . .	81
Camp Cookery	. . . .	81
How to Make a Fire by Rubbing Sticks	. . . . .	84
What to Do when Lost	. . . .	89
First Aid to the Injured	. . . .	93
The Stars, etc.	. . . .	99
Finding Latitude by Stars	. . . .	113
Sundial	. . . .	114
Archery	. . . .	115
Building a Log-cabin	. . . .	122
Teepees	. . . .	128
Knots	. . . .	134
Tracking or Trailing	. . . .	136
American Dialects	. . . .	139

PART IV—THE GAMES
(Copyright 1906, except those marked B. P.)

Deer-hunting	. . . .	140
The Bear Hunt	. . . .	143
Spearing the Great Sturgeon	. . . .	144
Tilting in the Water	. . . .	146
Canoe Tag	. . . .	147
Scouting	. . . .	147
The Game of Quicksight	. . . .	148
Far-sight, or Spot-the-rabbit	. . . .	149
Pole-Star	. . . .	149
Rabbit Hunt	. . . .	150
Hostile Spy	. . . .	150
The Man-hunt	. . . .	151
Hunt the Coon	. . . .	152
Spear-fights	. . . .	152
Navajo Feather-dance	. . . .	152
Feather Football	. . . .	153
Cock-fighting	. . . .	153
Hand-wrestling	. . . .	153
Badger-pulling	. . . .	153
Poison	. . . .	154
Hat-ball	. . . .	154
Duck-on-a-Rock	. . . .	154
Roadside Cribbage	. . . .	155
The War Dance	. . . .	156
The Fire-fly Dance	. . . .	158

(B. P.)

Lion Hunting	. . . .	163
Plant Race	. . . .	163

PAGE

Throwing the Assegai 164
Flag Raiding 164
Stalking and Reporting 165
"Spider and Fly" 166
How to Teach Stalking 166
Scout Hunting 167
Relay Race 167
Stalking 167
Track Memory 167
Spot the Thief 168
"Smugglers over the Border" 168
Shop Window 169
Shop Window (Indoors) 169
Follow the Trail 169
Scout's Nose 170
Scout Meets Scout 170
Shoot Out 170
Kim's Game 171
Morgan's Game 172
Snow Fort 172
Siberian Man Hunt 172

PART V—THE HONORS

CLASS I—RED HONORS

Heroism 174
Riding 174
General Athletics, by J. E. Sullivan and Dr. L. H. Gulick . . . 174
Athletic Specialties 178
Long-distance Athletics, by J. E. Sullivan and Dr. L. H. Gulick . 178
Water-sports and Travel 179
Mountain-climbing, by Sir Martin Conway 181
Target-shooting 182
Eyesight 183
Big-game Hunting 183

CLASS II—WHITE HONORS

Campercraft and Scouting 185
Archery, by Will H. Thompson 187
Long Range, Clout, or Flight Shooting 188
Fishing, by Dr. Henry van Dyke 188
Bait-casting, by Lou S. Darling 189

CLASS III—BLUE HONORS

Nature Study—Vertebrates, by Frank M. Chapman 190
Nature Study—Lower forms of life, by John Burroughs . . . 190
Geology, by Prof. Charles D. Walcott 191
Photography, by A. Radclyffe Dugmore 192

PREFACE

My various papers on Woodcraft and Scouting, herein col-
lected, appeared first, chiefly, in *Forest and Stream*, 1886 to 1893;
St. Nicholas, 1887 to 1890; *Scribner's*, 1892 and 4; *Century*,
1900; *The Ladies' Home Journal*, 1902, 3, and 4, and in *Country
Life*, 1903, 4, and 5. Acknowledgment is made to the editors of
these magazines.

The Woodcraft and Scouting movement that I aimed to
foster began to take shape in America some ten years ago. Because the idealized Indian of Hiawatha has always stood as the
model for outdoor life, woodcraft, and scouting, I called its
brotherhood the "Woodcraft Indians." In 1904 I went to
England to carry on the work there, and, knowing General R.
S. S. Baden-Powell as the chief advocate of scouting in the
British Army, invited him to coöperate in making the movement
popular. Accordingly, in 1908 he organized his Boy Scout
movement, incorporating the principles of the Indians with
other ethical features bearing on savings banks, fire drills, etc.,
as well as by giving it a partly military organization, and a carefully compiled and fascinating handbook.

All of the last that is applicable in America has been included
here, with due credit to General Sir Robert Baden-Powell, and
combined with the Birch-Bark Roll.

The present issue will constitute the Book of Organization.

It will be followed by others, making a dictionary of Woodcraft, with descriptions of the common trees, herbs, flowers, etc.,
trailing or tracking, sign-language, bird-stuffing, emergency foods,
first aid, lasso, boat-building, camp-fire songs and plays, and
many other things that belong to camp and outdoor life.

INTRODUCTION

E VERY American boy, a hundred years ago, lived either on a farm or in such close touch with farm life that he reaped its benefits. He had all the practical knowledge that comes from country surroundings; that is, he could ride, shoot, skate, run, swim; he was handy with tools; he knew the woods; he was physically strong, self-reliant, resourceful, well-developed in body and brain. In addition to which, he had a good moral training at home. He was respectful to his superiors, obedient to his parents, and altogether the best material of which a nation could be made.

We have lived to see an unfortunate change. Partly through the growth of immense cities, with the consequent specialization of industry, so that each individual has been required to do one small specialty and shut his eyes to everything else, with the resultant perpetual narrowing of the mental horizon.

Partly through the decay of small farming, which would have offset this condition, for each mixed farm was a college of handicraft.

And partly through the stereotyped forms of religion losing their hold, we see a very different type of youth in the country to-day.

It is the exception when we see a boy respectful to his superiors and obedient to his parents. It is the rare exception, now, when we see a boy that is handy with tools and capable of taking care of himself under all circumstances. It is the very, very rare exception when we see a boy whose life is absolutely governed by the safe old moral standards.

The personal interest in athletics has been largely superseded by an interest in spectacular games, which, unfortunately, tend to divide the nation into two groups—the few overworked champions in the arena, and the great crowd, content to do nothing but sit on the benches and look on, while indulging their tastes for tobacco and alcohol.

It is this last that is turning so many thoughtful ones against baseball, football, etc. This, it will be seen, is a reproduction of the condition that ended in the fall of Rome. In her days of growth, every man was a soldier; in the end, a few great gladiators were in the arena, to be watched and applauded by the millions who personally knew nothing at all of fighting or heroism.

Degeneracy is the word.

To combat the system that has turned such a large proportion of our robust, manly, self-reliant boyhood into a lot of flat-chested cigarette-smokers, with shaky nerves and doubtful vitality, I began the Woodcraft movement in America. Without saying as much, it aimed to counteract the evils attendant on arena baseball, football, and racing, by substituting the better, cleaner, saner pursuits of Woodcraft and Scouting. Its methods were fairly successful; at least 100,000 young people joined. But the idea, as enlarged by General Sir Robert Baden-Powell, has in less time achieved greater popularity in England; the results have been such that we are justified in adopting his innovations.

" Something to do, something to think about, something to enjoy in the woods, with a view always to character-building, for manhood, not scholarship, is the first aim of education." Introduction to third edition of " Birch-Bark Roll," 1904.

INTRODUCTION TO THE EARLY EDITIONS OF
THE BIRCH-BARK ROLL.

This is a time when the whole nation is turning toward the Outdoor Life, seeking in it the physical regeneration so needful for continued national existence—is waking to the fact long known to thoughtful men, that those live longest who live nearest to the ground, that is, who live the simple life of primitive times, divested, however, of the evils that ignorance in those times begot.

Consumption, the white man's plague since he has become a house race, is vanquished by the sun and air, and many ills of the mind also are forgotten, when the sufferer boldly takes to the life in tents.

Half our diseases are in our minds and half in our houses. We can safely leave the rest to the physicians for treatment.

Sport is the great incentive to Outdoor Life; nature study is the intellectual side of sport.

I should like to lead this whole nation into the way of living outdoors for at least a month each year, reviving and expanding a custom that as far back as Moses was deemed essential to the national well-being.

Not long ago a benevolent rich man, impressed with this idea, chartered a steamer and took some hundreds of slum boys up to the Catskills for a day in the woods. They were duly landed and told to " go in now and have a glorious time." It was like gathering up a netful of catfish and throwing them into the woods, saying, " Go and have a glorious time."

The boys sulked around and sullenly disappeared. An hour later, on being looked up, they were found in groups under the bushes, smoking cigarettes, shooting " craps," and playing cards, —the only things they knew.

Thus the well-meaning rich man learned that it is not enough to take men out-of-doors. We must also teach them to enjoy it.

The purpose of this Roll is to show how Outdoor Life may be followed to advantage.

Nine leading principles are kept in view:

(1) This movement is essentially for *recreation*.

(2) *Camp-life*. Camping is the simple life reduced to actual practice, as well as the culmination of the outdoor life.

Camping has no great popularity to-day, because men have the idea that it is possible only after an expensive journey to the wilderness; and women that it is inconvenient, dirty, and dangerous.

These are errors. They have arisen because camping as an art is not understood. When intelligently followed camp-life must take its place as a cheap and delightful way of living, as well as a mental and physical saviour of those strained and broken by the grind of the over-busy world.

The wilderness affords the ideal camping, but many of the benefits can be got by living in a tent on a town lot, piazza, or even house-top.

(3) *Self-government*. Control from without is a poor thing when you can get control from within. As far as possible, then, we make these camps self-governing. Each full member has a vote in affairs.

(4) *The Magic of the Camp-fire*. What is a camp without a camp-fire?—no camp at all, but a chilly place in a landscape, where some people happen to have some things.

When first the brutal anthropoid stood up and walked erect—was man, the great event was symbolized and marked by the lighting of the first camp-fire.

For millions of years our race has seen in this blessed fire the means and emblem of light, warmth, protection, friendly gathering, council. All the hallow of the ancient thoughts, hearth, fireside, home, is centred in its glow, and the home-tie itself is weakened with the waning of the home-fire. Not in the steam radiator can we find the spell; not in the water coil; not even in the gas-log: they do not reach the heart. Only the ancient sacred fire of wood has power to touch and thrill the chords of primitive remembrance. When men sit together at the camp-fire, they seem to shed all modern form and poise, and hark back to the primitive—to meet as man and man—to show the naked soul. Your camp-fire partner wins your love, or hate, mostly your love; and having camped in peace together, is a lasting bond of union,—however wide your worlds may be apart.

The camp-fire, then, is the focal centre of all primitive brotherhood. We shall not fail to use its magic powers.

(5) *Woodcraft Pursuits.* Realizing that *manhood, not scholarship,* is the first aim of education, we have sought out those pursuits which develop the finest character, the finest physique, and which may be followed out of doors, which, in a word, *make for manhood.*

By nearly every process of logic we are led primarily to Woodcraft, that is, Woodcraft in its largest sense,—meaning every accomplishment of an all-round Woodman:—Riding, Hunting, Camper-craft, Scouting, Mountaineerng, Indian-craft, Star-craft, Signalling, and Boating. To this we add all good Outdoor Athletics and Sports, including Sailing and Motoring, and Nature-Study, of which Wild Animal Photography is an important branch, but above all, Heroism.

About one hundred and fifty deeds or exploits are recognized in these various departments, and the members are given decorations that show what they achieved.

(6) *Honors by Standards.* The competitive principle is responsible for much that is evil. We see it rampant in our colleges to-day, where every effort is made to discover and develop a champion, while the great body of students is neglected. That is, the ones who are in need of physical development do not get it, and those who do not need it are over-developed. The result is much unsoundness of many kinds. A great deal of this would be avoided if we strove to bring all the individuals up to a certain standard. In our non-competitive tests the enemies are not "*the other fellows,*" but *time and space,* the forces of Nature. We try *not to down the others,* but *to raise ourselves.* A thorough application of this principle would end many of the evils now demoralizing college athletics. Therefore, all our honors are bestowed according to world-wide standards. (Prizes are not honors.)

(7) *Personal Decoration for Personal Achievements.* The love of glory is the strongest motive in a savage. Civilized man is supposed to find in high principle his master impulse. But those who believe that the men of our race, not to mention boys,

are civilized in this highest sense, would be greatly surprised if confronted with figures. Nevertheless, a human weakness may be good material to work with. I face the facts as they are. All have a chance for glory through the standards, and we blazon it forth in personal decorations that all can see, have, and desire.

(8) *A Heroic Ideal.* The boy from ten to fifteen, like the savage, is purely physical in his ideals. I do not know that I ever met a boy that would not rather be John L. Sullivan than Darwin or Tolstoi. Therefore, I accept the fact, and seek to keep in view an ideal that is physical, but also clean, manly, heroic, already familiar, and leading with certainty to higher things.

(9) *Picturesqueness in Everything.* Very great importance should be attached to this. The effect of the picturesque is magical, and all the more subtle and irresistible because it is not on the face of it reasonable. The charm of titles and gay costumes, of the beautiful in ceremony, phrase, dance, and song, are utilized in all ways.

THE AMERICAN FLAG

Saluting the Flag

It is generally agreed that the unmilitary salute of the flag is thus: Remove the hat, holding it in the left hand, which is straight down; place the right hand on the heart, and bow the head slightly.

HISTORY OF THE FLAG

These facts are derived chiefly from Canby & Balderston's "Evolution of the American Flag," 1909

October 9, 1774, General Washington wrote, "No such thing [as independence] is desired by any thinking man in America."

The first Continental flag appears to have been that flown at Cambridge, January 1, 1776. It consisted of thirteen bars, red and white, for the thirteen states, and in the corner had the Union Jack, for, up to that time, most Americans expected a friendly settlement with Great Britain. It was known as the Grand Union Flag.

King George's ill-advised ultimatum, received early in January, 1776, put a new color on affairs, and Washington, apparently for the first time, accepted the idea of complete independence, January 4, 1776. This necessitated a new flag without the symbol of British sovereignty.

There is little doubt that Washington himself designed or assisted to design the new flag, and about the 1st of June, 1776, General Washington, Committee Chairman Robert Morris, and Colonel George Ross, went to the upholstery of Betsy Ross, at No. 239 Arch Street, Philadelphia, and placed the order for the new flag. It consisted of the thirteen stripes, red and white, and thirteen six-pointed stars in a circle, white on a blue ground, to replace the Union Jack. Betsy Ross pointed out that the more pleasing five-rayed star could be cut by one clip of the scissors on the folded stuff. They accepted her amendment and the flag was made.

It was used thenceforth as the country's emblem, but not formally indorsed by Congress until a year later, when the following appears in the Journal of Congress:—

"June 14, 1777. *Resolved,* That the Flag of the United States be 13 stripes, alternately red and white; that the Union be 13 stars, white, in a blue field, representing a new Constellation."

On May 1, 1795, to represent also Vermont and Kentucky, both stars and stripes were increased to 15. In 1818, the admission of Tennessee, Ohio, Louisiana, Indiana, and Mississippi, called for further change. On July 4 of that year the number of stars was increased to 20, but, at the same time, the number of stripes was reduced to the original 13, and a further provision made for the addition of one star for each new State entering the Union, such addition to take effect on the 4th of July next succeeding such admission; so that the present number of stars is 48.

"The Star-Spangled Banner" was written by Francis Scott Key, during the bombardment of Fort McHenry by the British, September 13, 1814. It is usually considered the American National Anthem.

The text is as follows:—

THE STAR-SPANGLED BANNER

Oh, say, can you see, by the dawn's early light,
  What so proudly we hailed at the twilight's last gleaming—
Whose broad stripes and bright stars, through the perilous fight,
  O'er the ramparts we watched were so gallantly streaming!
And the rocket's red glare, the bombs bursting in air,
Gave proof through the night that our flag was still there;
Oh, say, does that star-spangled banner yet wave
O'er the land of the free and the home of the brave?

On that shore dimly seen through the mists of the deep,
  Where the foe's haughty host in dread silence reposes,
What is that which the breeze, o'er the towering steep,
  As it fitfully blows, now conceals, now discloses?
Now it catches the gleam of the morning's first beam,
In full glory reflected now shines on the stream;
'Tis the star-spangled banner; Oh, long may it wave
O'er the land of the free and the home of the brave!

And where is that band who so vauntingly swore
  That the havoc of war and the battle's confusion
A home and a country should leave us no more?
  Their blood has washed out their foul footsteps' pollution.
No refuge could save the hireling and slave
From the terror of flight, or the gloom of the grave;
And the star-spangled banner in triumph doth wave
O'er the land of the free and the home of the brave.

Oh, thus be it ever, when freemen shall stand
  Between their loved homes and the war's desolation!
Blest with victory and peace, may the heav'n-rescued land
  Praise the power that hath made and preserved us a nation.
Then conquer we must, when our cause it is just,
And this be our motto—"*In God is our trust;*"
And the star-spangled banner in triumph shall wave
O'er the land of the free and the home of the brave.

PART I. ORGANIZATION

Adopted with little change from Baden-Powell

BOY SCOUTS' ORGANIZATION

It is not intended that boy scouts should necessarily form a new corps separated from all others, but the boys who belong to any kind of existing organization, such as schools, football clubs, Boys' or Church Lads' Brigades, factories, district messengers, Telegraph Service, Cadet Corps, etc., etc., can *also* take up scouting in addition to their other work or play—especially on Saturdays or Sundays.

By scouting on Sundays I do not mean boys to go rampaging around, but to carry out nature-study of plants and animals, that is, of God's work in nature, and to do good turns.

But where there are any boys who do not belong to any kind of organization, they can form themselves into Patrols.

For this purpose officers are necessary.

Chief Scout. The head officer of all the boy scouts in the country is called the *Chief Scout.*

A Scout Commissioner is an official authorized to organize branches, to inspect troops, and generally to help scoutmasters.

A Scoutmaster is an officer who has charge of a troop. A troop consists of two or more patrols. Scouts address the scoutmaster as " Sir."

An Adjutant is an assistant scoutmaster.

A Chaplain is a clergyman or priest appointed to develop the religious training of a troop.

A Patrol Leader is a scout appointed by a scoutmaster or by vote of the patrol to command a patrol for one year. A patrol consists of six or eight scouts. Any patrol leader

8

who learns scouting from this book can train his boys to
be scouts.

A Corporal is a scout selected by the patrol leader to be his
assistant, and to take command of the patrol when he
himself is away.

A Scout, who must be between the ages of 12 and 18, is of
three kinds—first-class, second-class, and tenderfoot. A
first-class scout is one who has passed certain tests to
show that he is able to scout.

A Second-class Scout is one who has passed certain easy
tests in scouting.

A Tenderfoot is a boy who has joined the Boy Scouts, but
has not yet passed his tests for second-class scout. In
special cases boys of nine years old may become tenderfeet.

A Court of Honor is formed of the scoutmaster and two
patrol leaders, or in the case of a single patrol by the
patrol leader and the corporal. It decides rewards, pun-
ishments, and other questions.

Thus the whole organization consists of :—

The **Chief Scout.**

Scout Councils in each State or large city, composed of leading men, Scoutmasters, and others interested in the movement,
and representatives of other organizations for boys in the area,
to advise local committees. With Scout Commissioner appointed
by Chief Scout and Council as Honorary Secretary of Scout
Council, Inspector, and responsible to Headquarters for the
movement in his area.

Local Committees in each town and vicinity, or group of villages, composed of scoutmasters, and others interested in work
among boys in the district, to assist scoutmasters and develop
the movement. With Local Secretary to keep register and report to Scout Commissioner.

Troops, containing three or more patrols.

Patrols, containing six to eight scouts.

Scouts.

LOCAL ORGANIZATION

Local Committees, formed of scoutmasters and others interested in work among boys, are organized for every town and its
neighborhood, or group of villages, whose chief duties are:
    1. To appoint scoutmasters.
    2. To recognize and register troops and patrols.
    3. To award badges.
    Further, each county or city, or very large district, will have
its *Scout Council,* on which the Local Committees in its area
will be represented.
    The chief duties of the Scout Council are:—
    1. To promote generally the welfare of the Boy Scout Move-
       ment in its area.
    2. To secure as far as possible uniformity of policy among
       the Local Committees.
    Further details of the Local Scout Organizations, their head-
quarters, their work, etc., can be obtained from
              The Managing Secretary,
                  124 East Twenty-eighth Street,
                           New York.

POWER OF SCOUTMASTERS

    A scoutmaster has the power to enrol scouts and to recom-
mend them to the Local Committee for badges and medals.
He also has the power to release a scout from his oath, and to
withdraw his badges and discharge him. A scout who considers
himself unjustly treated may appeal to the Local Committee;
their decision will be final.
    A scout discharged for misconduct, or who deserts from his
troop or patrol, is no longer entitled to wear the uniform or
badges of the Boy Scouts.
    Scoutmasters will not accept as recruits boys from other
organizations, unless by desire of their officer.
    A scoutmaster appoints his own patrol leaders for one year,
when he can either reappoint them or substitute others. He can
at any time reduce a patrol leader to corporal or to scout.

TESTS FOR SCOUTS' BADGES

TENDERFOOT

A boy on joining the Boy Scouts must be 12 years old and pass a test in the following points :—
Before taking the Oath.
> Know the scout's laws and signs, and salute.
> Know the history of the Stars and Stripes.
> Tie four standard knots.

He then takes the scout's oath, and is enrolled as a Tenderfoot, and is entitled to wear the buttonhole badge.

SECOND-CLASS SCOUT

Before being awarded the second-class scout's badge a Tenderfoot must pass the following tests :—

1. Have at least one month's service as a Tenderfoot.
2. Elementary first aid and bandaging.
3. Signalling, elementary knowledge of semaphore, Myer or Morse alphabet.
4. Track half a mile in twenty-five minutes; or, if in a town, describe satisfactorily the contents of one shop window out of four, observed for one minute each.
5. Go a mile in twelve minutes at " scout's pace."
6. Lay and light a fire, using not more than two matches.
7. Cook a quarter of a pound of meat and two potatoes without cooking utensils other than the regulation kit.
8. Have at least one dollar in a savings bank.
9. Know the sixteen principal points of the compass.

FIRST-CLASS SCOUT

Before being awarded a first-class scout's badge a scout must pass the following tests, in addition to the tests laid down for second-class scouts :—

1. Swim fifty yards. (N.B.—This may be omitted where the doctor certifies that bathing is dangerous to the boy's health, in which case he must run a mile in eight minutes, or perform some equivalent selected by the scoutmaster.)
2. Must have two dollars at least in the savings bank.
3. Signalling. Send and receive a message either in semaphore, Myer or Morse, sixteen letters per minute.
4. Go on foot, or row a boat, alone to a point seven miles away and return again; or if conveyed by any vehicle, or animal, go to a distance of fifteen miles and back, and write a short report on it. It is preferable that he should take two days over it.
5. Describe or show the proper means for saving life in case of two of the following accidents (allotted by the examiners) : Fire, drowning, runaway carriage, sewer gas, ice-breaking, *or* bandage an injured patient, or revive apparently drowned person.
6. Cook satisfactorily two out of the following dishes, as may be directed : Porridge, bacon, hunter's stew; *or* skin and cook a rabbit, or pluck and cook a bird.
   Also
   Make a " damper " or camp sinker of half a pound of flour, or a " twist " baked on a thick stick.
7. Read a map correctly, and draw an intelligible rough sketch map. Point out a compass direction without the help of a compass.
8. Use an axe for felling or trimming light timber, or *as alternative,* produce an article of carpentry or joinery, or metal work, made by himself satisfactorily.
9. Judge distance, size, numbers, and height within 25 per cent. error.
10. Bring a tenderfoot trained by himself in the points required for a tenderfoot. (This may in special cases be postponed, when recruits are not immediately desired, but must be carried out within three months, or the badge withdrawn.)

TESTS FOR BADGES

The idea underlying the award of the badges is to offer to the young scout continual inducements for further improving himself, e.g. from second- to first-class scout, and then on to pioneering, signalling, life-saving, and so on.

The mistake usually made is for scoutmasters and examiners to require too high a standard of proficiency before awarding a badge. Our real object is to instil into *every* boy and encourage an idea of self-improvement. A fair average standard of proficiency is therefore all that is required. If you try higher than that you get a few brilliant boys qualified, but you dishearten a large number of others who fail, and you teach them the elements of hopelessness and helplessness, which is exactly what we want to avoid.

> [*Scoutmasters will remember that our policy is to get numbers. We don't want a select " corps d'élite," but we want to put a taste of the right spirit into every boy we can possibly get hold of. There are ten million boys wanting it.*]

BADGES

The scout's badge is this :—

The scout's badge is the arrow-head, which shows the north on a map or on the compass. It is the badge of the scout in the Army, because he shows the way; so, too, a peace scout shows the way in doing his duty and helping others.

The motto on it is the scout's motto of

" BE PREPARED,"

which means that a scout must always be prepared at any moment to do his duty, and to face danger in order to help his fellow-men. Its scroll is turned up at the ends like a scout's mouth, because he does his duty with a smile and willingly.

The knot is to remind the scout to do a good turn to some one daily.

A scout's badge represents and is called his " life." It is given him when he passes the tests in scout craft necessary to make him a scout.

If he breaks his word of honor, or otherwise disgraces himself, his life is taken (that is, his badge), and he is expelled from the patrol.

The badge, with a ring round it and a plume, is worn by scout-masters on the left side of the hat or cap.

The badge is worn by patrol leaders on front of the hat or cap.

The badge is worn by corporal on the left arm above elbow with a strip of white braid below it.

The badge is worn by scouts on the left arm above the elbow.

The badge worn by first-class scouts is the whole badge.

Only the motto part of the badge is worn by second-class scouts.

BADGES OF MERIT

[*First-class scouts who wish to obtain these Badges of Merit must pass the necessary tests before a Court of Honor, or before two qualified and independent examiners. The Ambulance Badge is worn on the right arm halfway between elbow and shoulder—the other badges are worn on the right arm, starting from the cuff upwards in the order in which they are gained.*]

These badges are only open to First-Class Scouts and Scout-masters.

Ambulance.
Fireman.   } Of public utility, and therefore worn at the top
Cyclist.   }   of the arm.

Clerk.   Seaman.   Stalker.   Electrician.
Signaller.   Marksman.   Gardener.   Musician.
Pioneer.   Master-at-Arms. Horseman.

SHOULDER LINES are awarded to any scout who gains any six of the above. The "SILVER WOLF" to any scouts who gain all fourteen.

"HONORARY SILVER WOLF" is granted in exceptional cases to individuals rendering specially valuable services to the Boy Scouts Movement.

AMBULANCE BADGE.—(To be worn halfway between elbow and shoulder on right arm.)

A scout must pass satisfactory tests as follows:—

AMBULANCE

Fireman's lift.
Drag insensible man with rope.
Improvise a stretcher.   Fling a life-line.
Show the position of the main arteries.
Demonstrate to stop bleeding from vein, artery, internal.
How to improvise splints, diagnose and bind fractured limb.
Give complete practice of artificial respiration.
Bandage a given injury.
Show how to deal with choking, or burning, poison, or grit in eye, as examiner may require.
Have a satisfactory general knowledge of laws of health and sanitation as given in "Scouting for Boys," including dangers of smoking, incontinence, want of ventilation, etc.

FIREMAN.—How to give the alarm to inhabitants, police, etc. How to enter burning buildings.   How to prevent spread of fire. Use of hose, unrolling, joining up; hydrants; use of nozzle, etc. Use of escape, ladders, and shutes; improvising ropes, jumping sheets, etc. "Fireman's Lift," dragging patient, working in fumes, etc. Use of fire-extinguishers. Rescue of animals. Salvage of property, climbing, bucket-passing. "Scrum" to keep back crowd.

CYCLING.—The scout must sign a certificate that he owns a bicycle in good working order, which he is willing to use for service of the Government in case of emergency, such as national defence, carrying despatches, etc. He must be able to repair punctures, etc., to read a map, and to repeat correctly a verbal message. On ceasing to own or to have certain use of a bicycle the scout must be required to hand back his badge.

CYCLING

His rank would be that of "Cyclist Scout."

CLERK.—Good handwriting and handprinting.

Use of typewriting machine. Write a few sentences from dictation.

Write a letter from memory on subject given verbally five minutes previously. Or *as alternative to the letter* draw a map or plan, or draw a picture from life or from memory.

Or *as alternative to all above* write in shorthand from dictation at twenty words a minute as minimum.

SIGNALLER.—Pass tests in both sending and receiving messages in semaphore and in Morse or Myer. Not less than twenty-four letters per minute.

SIGNALLING

To give and read signals by sound.

To make correct smoke and flame signals with fires.

To give the proper signals (as in infantry training) to show the presence of enemy, etc.

PIONEER.—Extra efficiency in pioneering in the following tests or suitable equivalents :—

Felling a nine-inch tree, or scaffolding pole, neatly and quickly.

Tie eight kinds of knots quickly in the dark or blindfolded.

Build model bridge or derrick.

Lash spars properly together for scaffolding.

Make a camp kitchen.

Build a hut suitable for three occupants.

PIONEERING

Or as alternative.—Make a table, chair, or cupboard, or two boxes with locks without assistance.

SEAMAN.—Tie eight knots rapidly in the dark or blindfolded.

Fling a rope coil.

Row a boat single-handed, and punt it with pole, or scull it over the stern. Steer a boat rowed by others. Bring a boat properly alongside and make it fast.

SEAMANSHIP   Box the compass. Read a chart.

State direction by the stars and sun.

Weather wisdom and knowledge of tides.

Swim fifty yards with trousers, socks, and shirt on.

Climb a rope or pole of fifteen feet; or, *as alternative,* dance the hornpipe correctly.

Sew and darn a shirt and trousers.

Understand the general principle of marine engines, and steam or hydraulic winch.

Knowledge of the different national flags and rigs of sailing vessels and classes of men-of-war.

MARKSMAN.—Pass the following tests for miniature rifle shooting:—

MARKSMANSHIP

Score not less than 114 points in 30 shots.

The 30 shots may all be fired at 20, 25, 50, or 100 yards, or in a series of 10 at each of three distances, or in a series of 10 at one distance and a series of 20 at another distance, but not of necessity on the same day.

N. R. A. standard targets to be used.

Scoring: Bull's Eye, 5 points; Inner, 4 points; Magpie, 3 points; Outer, 2 points.

Or as alternative.—Pass the tests for shooting with the crossbow. See Scout Chart, No. 17. Price 15c., post-free.

Also.—Judge distance on unknown ground: five distances between 50 and 300 yards, five between 300 and 600 yards, with not more than an error of 15 per cent. on the average.

MASTER-AT-ARMS.—Proficiency in three out of these six subjects: Single stick, boxing, ju jitsu, wrestling, quarter staff, and fencing.

MASTER-OF-ARMS

STALKERS.—Series of twenty photographs of wild animals or wild birds taken from life by the scout, and all developed and printed by himself.

Or alternative.—A collection made by the scout himself of sixty species of wild flowers, ferns, or grasses, dried and mounted, and correctly named.

STALKER'S

Or alternative.—Colored drawings of twenty flowers, ferns, or grasses, or twelve sketches from life of animals or birds; all must be done by the scout himself, and original sketches, as well as finished pictures, must be submitted.

Or alternative.—Be able to name sixty different kinds of animals, insects, reptiles, or birds in a museum or zoölogical garden, and give particulars of the lives and habits, appearance and markings of twenty of them.

GARDENER.—Dig and measure a bit of ground not less than twelve feet square.

Know the names of a dozen plants pointed out in an ordinary garden.

Understand what is meant by pruning, grafting, and manuring.

Plant and grow successfully six kinds of vegetables, plants, or flowers from seeds or cuttings.

Cut and make a walking-stick, or cut grass with scythe under supervision.

HORSEMAN.—Ability to ride at all paces, and to jump an ordinary fence on horseback.

To saddle and bridle a horse correctly.

To harness a horse correctly in single or double harness, and to drive.

To understand how to water and feed, and to what amount.

To groom a horse properly.

To understand the evil of bearing and hame reins, and ill-fitting saddlery. To know lameness and its principal causes and remedies.

ELECTRICIAN.—Knowledge of method of rescue and of resuscitation of person insensible from shock.

Ability to make simple electro-magnet, elementary knowledge of action of simple battery cells, and the working of electric bells and telephone.

To understand and remedy fusing wire. To repair broken electric connections.

MUSICIAN.—Ability to play an instrument that would be of use in a band or orchestra (other than drum or triangle). And to read simple music.

Or to play drum properly, *and* any kind of musical instrument or toy such as penny whistle, mouth organ, etc., *and* sing a song.

MEDALS

BRONZE AND SILVER CROSS
FOR SAVING LIFE

MEDAL OF MERIT

For meritorious deeds.. To obtain one of these will be the ambition of every scout.

These medals are only granted by the Chief Scout, or by the Scout President in a colony, on special recommendation from the patrol leader or scoutmaster, who should send in a full account of the case through the local committee if one exists.

These are worn on the right breast, and are awarded as follows:—

BRONZE CROSS (Red Ribbon).—For saving life at risk to own.

SILVER CROSS (Blue Ribbon).—For saving life or helping to save life without risk to self, but where life might have been lost.

(GILT) MEDAL OF MERIT (White Ribbon).—For meritorious service, assisting police at personal risk, or for *twenty* various good deeds, such as stopping a runaway horse, helping at a fire, etc. Full proof of each deed must be supplied. Records should be kept by scoutmasters until the twenty are complete; then they should be sent up to the headquarters.

" The Silver Wolf."—The Red Indians of North America call their best scout " Gray Wolf," because the gray wolf is a beast that sees everything and yet is never seen, and is brave and untiring.

Mr. E. Thompson Seton, of the Boy Scouts in America, is called " Black Wolf."

And the fighting tribes in South Africa in the same way speak of a scout as a wolf.

So in the Boy Scouts a special badge and title of " Silver Wolf " will be given as a reward for very special distinction in scouting. See *ante,* Badges of Merit.

All medals and badges are only worn as above when scouts are on duty or in camp. At other times they should be worn on the right breast of the waistcoat, underneath the jacket.

A small arrow-head badge may be worn at all times in the button-hole.

Scoutmasters can wear any badges for which they qualify.

They do not wear first-class scout badges, as it is understood by their rank that they are scouts.

It should be noted that the rules given in this book are generally intended to apply to units of Boy Scouts which do not belong to existing organizations. Where scouting is taken up by any society, such, for instance, as the Boys' Brigade, that society takes up as much or as little as it likes of the training. Its own officers will be considered to be scoutmasters without further recommendation, and the boys who take up scouting keep to the uniform of their corps, and do not wear Boy Scout uniform or badges unless their officers permit it.

If it is desired that such boys should wear scouts' uniform, the officers will be expected to work in conjunction with the local Boy Scout Committee; and if the officers wish for scoutmaster warrants or the boys to wear the scouts' badges, life-saving medals, or badges of merit, they must pass the same tests as other scoutmasters or boy scouts.

Distinction for Boy Scouts.—A boy scout when signing his name officially to any letter or document on scout business is entitled to put after his signature any distinctions which he may have gained, by drawing a small sketch of the badge.

Thus, if he is a first-class scout, who has passed in signalling and seamanship, he signs thus :—

James Harding ⚓ ✕ ⚓

Similarly, these signs may be shown after his name in official lists, etc.

THE SCOUT'S OATH

Before he becomes a scout a boy must take the scout's oath, thus :—
"I give my word of honor that I will do my best
1. To do my duty to God and my country.
2. To help other people at all times.
3. To obey the Scout Law."
(For Scout Law, see p. 32.)
When taking this oath the scout will stand, holding his right hand raised level with his shoulder, palm to the front, thumb resting on the nail of the little finger, and the other three fingers upright, pointing upward :—
This is the scout's salute and secret sign.
When the hand is raised shoulder high it is called "The Half Salute."
When raised to the forehead it is the "Full Salute."

SCOUT'S SALUTE AND SECRET SIGN

The three fingers held up (like the three points of the scout's badge) remind him of his three promises in the scout's oath.
1. Honor God and the country.
2. Help others.
3. Obey the Scout Law.
When a scout meets another for the first time in the day, whether he is a comrade or a stranger, he salutes with the secret sign in the half salute.

He always salutes an officer—that is, a patrol leader, or a scoutmaster, or any commissioned officer of the national forces, army and navy—with the full salute.

Also the hoisting of the Stars and Stripes, the colors of a regiment, the playing of the National Anthem, and any funeral.

A scout who has the " Silver Wolf " honor is entitled to make the sign with the first finger and thumb opened out, the remaining fingers clenched, thumb upwards. This is a sign with the Red Indians of America.

A man told me the other day that " he was an Englishman, and just as good as anybody else, and he was blowed if ever he would raise a finger to salute his so-called ' betters '; he wasn't going to be a slave and kow-tow to them, not he! " and so on. That is a churlish spirit, which is very common among fellows who have not been brought up as scouts.

I didn't argue with him, but I might have told him that he had got hold of the wrong idea about saluting.

A salute is merely a sign between men of standing. It is a privilege to be able to salute any one.

In the old days the free men of England all were allowed to carry weapons, and when they met each other each would hold up his right hand to show that he had no weapon in it, and that they met as friends. So also when an armed man met a defence-less person or a lady.

Slaves or serfs were not allowed to carry weapons, and so had to slink past the freemen without making any sign.

Nowadays people do not carry weapons; but those who would have been entitled to do so, such as knights, esquires, and men-at-arms, that is, any living on their own property or earning their own living, still go through the form of saluting each other by holding up their hand to their cap, or even taking it off.

" Wasters " are not entitled to salute, and so should slink by, as they generally do, without taking notice of the free men or wage-earners.

To salute merely shows that you are a right sort of fellow and mean well to the other; there is nothing slavish about it.

If a stranger makes the scout's sign to you, you should acknowledge it at once by making the sign back to him, and then shake hands with the LEFT HAND. If he then shows his scout's badge, or proves that he is a scout, you must treat him as a brother-scout, and help him in any way you can.

SCOUT'S UNIFORM

If you already belong to a corps which has a uniform, you dress in that uniform; but on passing the tests for a scout given here you wear the scout badge, if your commanding officer allows it, in addition to any of your corps' badges that you may have won.

Scouts in a patrol should, as far as possible, dress alike, especially as regards hats and neckerchief and color of shirt or sweater.

If your patrol does not belong to any uniformed corps, it should dress as nearly as possible thus:—

HAT.—Khaki color, flat brim and chin strap.

NECKERCHIEF. — Of the colors of your patrol; the neckerchief is worn knotted at the throat and also at the

SCOUT'S UNIFORM
PATROL LEADER WITH SCOUT

ends, and is tied loosely round the neck.

SHIRT.—Flannel—blue, khaki, or gray. In winter a jersey or sweater of the same color, if preferred.

BREECHES.—Short khaki, gray or blue, with braid or cord on seam.

BELT.—Brown leather, two swivels, coat strap—pouch optional. Buckles, etc., should be of dull metal.

STOCKINGS.—Dark color or khaki, preferably turned down below the knee.

Shoes or Boots.—Brown or black, or brown sneaks.
Staff.—Marked in feet and inches. Not shod, as it is for
    feeling the way at night quietly.
Haversack.—Khaki color.
Shoulder-knot.—A bunch of ribbons or tapes of patrol
    color on left shoulder.
Whistle.—With cord round neck for patrol leaders and scout-
    masters.
Knife.—On lanyard and hitched to swivel on belt.
Nothing but the above should be worn visibly. All extras,
such as ropes, kettles, etc., to be carried in haversack. A scout's
clothing should be of flannel or wool, as much as possible; cot-
ton next the skin should be avoided, as it does not absorb the
perspiration, and is likely to give you a chill.

SCOUTMASTER'S UNIFORM FOR CAMP, GAMES, ETC.

Hat.—Flat-brimmed (khaki), with the badge on left side.
Shirt.—Khaki flannel scout's shirt, with khaki collar and
    green tie, short sleeves. Or the colored neckerchief may
    be worn. If needed, a white sweater may be worn over
    the shirt.
Shoulder-knot.—White on left shoulder.
Belts, Shoes, etc.—As for scouts.

FOR DRILLS AND PARADES

Hat, shirt (with colored collar and tie), belt as above, knicker
    breeches, khaki putties, laced shoes (preferably brown),
    walking-stick, whistle, and lanyard.
If a coat is needed, it should be a khaki or tweed one of the
Norfolk variety, and not an imitation of a military tunic. Such
things as spurs, swords, revolvers, gauntlets, and riding crops
should not be used.

ASSISTANT SCOUTMASTERS

The uniforms should be the same as scoutmasters'. The badge on the hat is the white metal one, and worn on the left side. The buttonhole badge is also white metal.

Corporal has a stripe of white braid three inches long stitched across his sleeve below the badge.

Scouts' War Songs

1. *The Scouts' chorus.*

 To be shouted on the march, or as applause at games, meetings, etc. Must be sung exactly in time.

 Leader: Een gonyâma—gonyâma.
 Chorus: Invooboo.
 Yah bô! Yah bô!
 Invooboo.

The meaning is—

 Leader: "He is a lion!"
 Chorus: "Yes! he is better than that; he is a hippopotamus!"

SOLO (*Leader*).   CHORUS.

Een - gon - yâm - a   Gon - yâm - a;   In - voo - boo!

Ya - Boh!   Ya - Boh!   In - voo - boo. . .

2. *The Scouts' Rally.*

 To be shouted as a salute, or in a game, or at any time.
 Leader: Be prepared!
 Chorus: Zing-a-Zing!
 Bom! Bom!
(Stamp or bang something at the "Bom! Bom!")

For scout master to call together his troop by bugle ; or for scout to whistle to attract attention of another scout.

NOTE TO INSTRUCTORS

Although the war dance and songs may seem at first sight to be gibberish—especially to those who have never had much to do with boys—yet there is a certain value underlying them.

If you want, for instance, to get discipline among your lads it means their constantly bottling up some energy that requires an occasional vent or safety-valve. A war dance supplies such vent, but still in a certain disciplined way.

Also it forms an attraction to wilder spirits who would never join a band of nice, quiet, good boys.

Mr. Tomlin, " the hooligan tamer," catches and gets his lads in hand entirely by the force of energetic singing and action in chorus.

Most schools and colleges have their " Ra-ra-ra " choruses, of which " Zing-a-zing: bom, bom " is a type.

The war dance or any kind of dance is of great value in giving the lads exercise in a confined space, and also in developing their activity and command of their feet, and in getting rid of awkward self-consciousness.

CRESTS, TOTEMS, OR PATROL SIGNS

Each troop is named after the place to which it belongs. Each patrol in that troop is named after an animal or bird. Thus the 33rd London Troop may have five patrols which are respectively the Wolves, the Ravens, the Curlews, the Bulls, the Owls.

BLUE BUFFALO.
1902.
On white ground.

FLYING EAGLES.
1902.
"*Yek-yek-yek.*"
Black and white on red.

BLUE HERONS.
1904.
"*Hrrrrr.*"
Blue on green.

HORNED
KINGBIRDS.
1902.

SINAWA.
1903.
Black on red.

BLACKBEARS.
1906.
Black on red.

AHMEEKS.
1909.

SILVER FOXES.
1904.

RED TRAILERS.
1903.

MOON BAND.
1905.
Yellow on blue.

OWENOKES.
1904.

BLAZING ARROW.

Each scout in a patrol has his regular number, the patrol leader being No. 1, the corporal No. 2, and the scouts have the consecutive numbers after these. Scouts usually work in pairs as comrades, Nos. 3 and 4 together, Nos. 5 and 6 together, and Nos. 7 and 8.

A white shoulder knot is worn by Officers, and Umpires at games.

Each scout in the patrol has to be able to make the call of his patrol-animal—thus every scout in the "Ravens" must be able to imitate the croak of the raven. This is the sign by which scouts of a patrol can communicate with each other when hiding

MONGOOSE.
Squeak—"Cheep."
BROWN AND ORANGE.

HAWK.
Cry (same as Eagle)
—"Kreeee." PINK.

WOLF.
Howl—"How-oooo."
YELLOW AND BLACK.

PEEWIT.
Whistle—"Teewitt.
GREEN AND WHITE.

HOUND.
Bark—"Bawow-wow."
ORANGE.

CAT.
Cry—"Meeaow."
GREY AND BROWN.

JACKAL.
Laughing Cry—"Wah-
wah-wah-wah-wah."
GREY AND BLACK.

RAVEN.
Cry—"Kar-kaw."
BLACK.

BUFFALO.
Lowing (same as Bull)
"Um-maouw."
RED AND WHITE.

PEACOCK.
Cry—"Bee-oik."
GREEN AND BLUE.

BULL.
Lowing—"Um-maouw."
RED.

SEAL.
Call—"Hark."
RED AND BLACK.

OWL.
Whistle—"Koot-koot-koo."
BLUE.

TIGER.
Purr—"Grrrao."
VIOLET.

LION.
Call—"Ed-ugh."
YELLOW AND RED.

KANGAROO.
Call—"Coo-ee."
RED AND GREY.

HORSE.
Whinny—"Hee-e-e-e."
BLACK AND WHITE.

FOX.
Bark—"Ha-ha."
YELLOW AND GREEN.

BEAR.
Growl—"Boorrr."
BROWN AND RED.

STAG.
Roar—"Baow."
VIOLET AND BLACK.

STORK.
Cry—"Korrr."
BLUE AND WHITE.

PANTHER.
Tongue in side of mouth—
"Kecook."
YELLOW.

CURLEW.
Whistle—"Curley."
GREEN.

HYENA.
Laughing Cry—
"Ooowah-oowah-wah."
BLACK AND BROWN.

RAM.
Bleat—"Ba-a-a."
BROWN.

WOOD PIGEON.
Call—"Book-hooroo."
BLUE AND GREY.

EAGLE.
Very shrill cry—"Kreeee."
GREEN AND BLACK

HIPPO.
Hiss—"Brrussssh."
PINK AND BLACK.

RATTLESNAKE.
Rattle a pebble in a small
potted meat tin.
PINK AND WHITE.

WILD BOAR.
Grunt—"Broof-broof."
GREY AND PINK.

COBRA.
Hiss—"Pssst."
ORANGE AND BLACK.

CUCKOO.
Call—"Cook-koo."
GREY.

OTTER.
Cry—"Hoi-oi-oick."
BROWN AND WHITE.

BEAVER.
Slap made by clapping
hands.
BLUE AND YELLOW.

or at night.   No scout is allowed to imitate the call of any patrol
except his own.   The patrol leader calls up the patrol at any time
by sounding his whistle and uttering the call of the patrol.

Also when a scout makes signs on the ground for others to
read he also draws the head of the patrol animal.   Thus if he
wants to show that a certain road should not be followed he
draws the sign across it, " Not to be followed," and adds the
head of his patrol animal to show which patrol discovered that
the road was no good, and his own number to the left of the head
to show which scout discovered it, thus:

Each patrol leader has a small white flag on his staff with
the head of his patrol animal shown in red cloth stitched on to
it on both sides.   Thus the " Wolves " of the 1st London Troop
would have the flag shown below.

All these signs scouts must be able to draw according to the
patrol to which they belong.

> [*Practise with chalk on floors or walls, or with a stick on
> sand or mud.*]

Scout signs on the ground or wall, etc., close to the right-hand
side of the road.

→   Road to be followed.

→   Letter hidden three paces from here in the direction
        of the arrow.

✕ This path not to be followed.

◉ " I have gone home."

(Signed) Patrol Leader of the Blackbears Fifteenth
Connecticut Troop.

At night sticks with a wisp of grass round them or stones should be laid on the road in similar forms so that they can be felt with the hand.

[*Practise this.*]

SCOUT LAW

Scouts, all the world over, have unwritten laws which bind them just as much as if they had been printed in black and white.

They come down to us from old times.

The Japanese have their Bushido, or laws of the old Samurai warriors, just as we have chivalry or rules of the knights of the Middle Ages. The Red Indians in America have their laws of honor; the Zulus, the natives of India, the European nations— all have their ancient codes.

The following are the rules which apply to Boy Scouts, and which you swear to obey when you take your oath as a Scout, so it is as well that you should know all about them.

The scouts' motto is:

BE PREPARED

which means you are always to be in a state of readiness in mind and body to do your DUTY.

Be Prepared in Mind by having disciplined yourself to be obedient to every order, and also by having thought out before-hand any accident or situation that might occur, so that you *know* the right thing to do at the right moment, and are willing to do it.

Be Prepared in Body by making yourself strong and active and *able* to do the right thing at the right moment, and do it.

THE SCOUT LAW

1. A Scout's Honor is to be Trusted.

   If a scout says " On my honor it is so," that means that it *is* so, just as if he had taken a most solemn oath.

   Similarly, if a scout officer says to a scout, " I trust you on your honor to do this," the scout is bound to carry out the order to the very best of his ability, and to let nothing interfere with his doing so.

   If a scout were to break his honor by telling a lie, or by not carrying out an order exactly when trusted on his honor to do so, he may be directed to hand over his scout badge, and never to wear it again.   He may also be directed to cease to be a scout.

2. A Scout is Loyal to the President, and to his officers, and to his parents, his country, and his employers.   He must stick to them through thick and thin against any one who is their enemy or who even talks badly of them.

3. A Scout's Duty is to be Useful and to Help Others.

   And he is to do his duty before anything else, even though he gives up his own pleasure, or comfort, or safety to do it.   When in difficulty to know which of two things to do, he must ask himself, " Which is my duty? " that is, " Which is best for other people? "—and do that one. He must Be Prepared at any time to save life, or to help injured persons.   And *he must try his best to do a good turn* to somebody every day.

4. A Scout is a Friend to All, and a Brother to Every Other Scout, no matter to what Social Class the Other Belongs.

   Thus if a scout meets another scout, even though a stranger to him, he must speak to him, and help him in any way that he can, either to carry out the duty he is then doing, or by giving him food, or, as far as possible, anything that he may be in want of.   A scout must never be a SNOB. A snob is one who looks down upon another because he is poorer, or who is poor and resents another because he is rich.   A scout accepts the other man as he finds him, and makes the best of him.

" Kim," the boy scout, was called by the Hindoos " Little friend of all the world," and that is the name that every scout should earn for himself.

5. A Scout is Courteous: That is, he is polite to all—but especially to women and children, and old people and invalids, cripples, etc. And he must not take any reward for being helpful or courteous.

6. A Scout is a Friend to Animals. He should save them as far as possible from pain, and should not kill any animal unnecessarily, even if it is only a fly—for it is one of God's creatures. Killing an animal for food is allowable.

7. A Scout Obeys Orders of his parents, patrol leader, or scoutmaster without question.

Even if he gets an order he does not like he must do as soldiers and sailors do, he must carry it out all the same *because it is his duty;* and after he has done it he can come and state any reasons against it : but he must carry out the order at once. That is discipline.

8. A Scout Smiles and Looks Pleasant under all circumstances. When he gets an order he should obey it cheerily and readily, not in a slow, hang-dog sort of way.

Scouts never grumble at hardships, nor whine at each other, nor swear when put out.

When you just miss a train, or some one treads on your favorite corn—not that a scout ought to have such things as corns—or under any annoying circumstances, you should force yourself to smile at once, and then whistle a tune, and you will be all right.

A scout goes about with a smile on. It cheers him and cheers other people, especially in time of danger, for he keeps it up then all the same.

The punishment for swearing or using bad language is for each offence a mug of cold water to be poured down the offender's sleeve by the other scouts. It was the punishment invented by the old British scout, Captain John Smith, three hundred years ago.

9. A Scout is Thrifty, that is, he saves every penny he can, and puts it into the bank, so that he may have money to

keep himself when out of work, and thus not make himself a burden to others; or that he may have money to give away to others when they need it.

NOTES FOR INSTRUCTORS

SUMMARY

A way by which scout officers can do a national good.

Bad citizenship, which ruined the Roman Empire, is creeping in among us to-day.

The future of our country will much depend on the character of the rising generation. For this too little is at present being done in the way of development in our schools.

Peace scouting is suggested as an attractive means towards developing character and good citizenship.

Can be carried out by young men of all kinds, without expense, each training a few boys.

Experiment has already been successful.

The county organization of boy scouts.

Hints to would-be instructors for carrying out the training, and for explaining it to others.

Books to read on the subject.

REASONS FOR THE BOY SCOUT SCHEME

It becomes part of the duty of any one who joins the Boy Scout movement as an official to get others also to interest themselves in it in a practical manner, because our object is to sow healthy seed not merely in a few thousand boys, but in a few million if possible.

For this purpose it is well that he should himself realize and be able to explain the aims and outside effects of our scheme.

NATIONAL DETERIORATION

In the first place we have to recognize that our nation is in need of help, from within, if it is to maintain its position as a leading factor for peace and prosperity among the other nations of the earth.

History shows us, that with scarcely an exception, every great nation, after climbing laboriously to the zenith of its power, has then apparently become exhausted by the effort, and has settled down in a state of repose, relapsing into idleness and into indifference to the fact that other nations were pushing up to destroy it, whether by force of arms or by the more peaceful but equally fatal method of commercial strangulation. In every case the want of some of that energetic patriotism which made the country has caused its ruin; in every case the verdict of history has been, " Death through bad citizenship."

Signs have not been wanting of recent years that all is not right with our citizenship in Britain. Ominous warnings have been heard from many authorities and many sources, in almost every branch of our national life. These have been recently summed up by one of our public men in the following words:—

" The same causes which brought about the fall of the great Roman Empire are working to-day in Great Britain."

THE UNEMPLOYED

One sign of the disease (which was also one of the signs of decay in Rome before her fall) is the horde of unemployed leading miserable, wasted lives in all parts of the country—the great army of drones in our hive.

It is no longer a mere temporary excrescence, but is a growing tumor pregnant with evil for the nation.

These people, *having never been taught to look after themselves, or to think of the future or their country's good,* allow themselves to become slaves by the persuasive power of a few professional agitators whose living depends on agitating (whether it is needed or not); and blinded by the talk of these men they spurn the hand which provides the money, till they force employers to spend fortunes either in devising machinery that will take their place and will not then go on strike, or in getting in foreign labor, or in removing their business to other countries, leaving the agitators fat, but the mass of their deluded followers unemployed and starving and unable to provide for the crowds of children which they still continue improvidently to bring into the world.

PLENTY OF OPENINGS, BUT FEW FITTED FOR THEM

Yet there is work for all and money for all in the country.

Mr. John Burns has emphasized this latter point.   If the men would be thrifty and give up beer and tobacco, which, after all, are luxuries and merely a matter of habit, there would be £189,000,000 available for the betterment of their families in the year.

But there is a demand for Britons, of the right sort, everywhere.   Our mercantile marine ships are being largely manned by foreigners; a great amount of foreign labor has to be used throughout England (there are said to be 100,000 German waiters alone) ; our colonies are eagerly in want of men; and yet England cannot supply them—at least, not of the sort that will be any good.

It is only when one travels out of Britain and sees what is going on in other countries and colonies, and compares notes with men of other nationalities, that one realizes the gravity of our national condition, as well as the possibilities that lie before us if we can rise to the occasion.   One cannot see these things within the narrow limits of England.

I write this on board a British ship which is carrying some 1200 white emigrants to Argentina.   Only three out of the 1200 are Englishmen—the rest are chiefly Italians and Spaniards.

I questioned several authorities on South America on the subject, and was told that several shiploads of Englishmen were brought out, but the experiment was not a success.   They could not face the outdoor life of the prairie, where they had to turn their hand to different kinds of jobs, such as building their own huts, cooking their own food, working with cattle or at agriculture, and so on.   No; they could not do without their public-house, their music-halls, and their football-betting, and so they drifted back to the towns and to England.   Russians, Germans, Italians, and Spaniards have now taken their place and are flowing into the country at the rate of some five thousand a week. They apply themselves energetically to their work, live in harmony with the other inhabitants, and are making for themselves happy and prosperous lives in this sunny land of promise. Australia wants emigrants; there is room in South Africa, but not for loafers.

Canada, with its enormous possibilities, is anxious for men, but its verdict, after trial of the British that have gone out there, is, " we are glad of the few good, thrifty, enterprising workers that have come, but we have no use for the majority that were sent, namely, fellows who :—

1. Had no idea of self-discipline.

2. Were generally surly and ready to grumble at difficulties.

3. Could not be relied upon to stick to a job the moment that it appeared at all irksome or distasteful to them."

And so foreigners are flocking in to reap the fruit in the colonies planted by us, while our own people loaf and suffer in slums at home.

FOOTBALL

One of the causes of the downfall of Rome was that the people, being fed by the State to the extent of three-quarters of the population, ceased to have any thought or any responsibility for themselves or their children, and consequently became a nation of unemployed wasters.   They frequented the circuses, where paid performers appeared before them in the arena, much as we see the crowds now flocking to look on at paid players playing football.

Football in itself is a grand game for developing a lad physically and also morally, for he learns to play with good temper and unselfishness, to play in his place and " play the game," and these are the best of training for any game of life.   But it is a vicious game when it draws crowds of lads away from playing the game themselves to be merely onlookers at a few paid per-formers. I yield to no one in enjoyment of the sight of those splendid specimens of our race, trained to perfection, and play-ing faultlessly; but my heart sickens at the reverse of the medal —thousands of boys and young men, pale, narrow-chested, hunched-up, miserable specimens, smoking endless cigarettes, numbers of them betting, all of them learning to be hysterical as they groan or cheer in panic unison with their neighbors— the worst sound of all being the hysterical scream of laughter that greets any little trip or fall of a player. One wonders whether this can be the same nation which had gained for itself the reputation of being a stolid manhood, unmoved by panic or excitement, and reliable in the tightest of places.

Get the lads away from this—teach them to be manly, to play the game, whatever it may be, and not be merely onlookers and loafers.

IS OUR DISEASE INCURABLE?

In the eyes of some, these and many similar signs appear to indicate that we have arrived at the point of our existence where we may fold our hands and resign our life. But is not national life very like that of the individual?

How many a man in the case of sickness has given up all hope of recovery and has accordingly died, whereas another, by carry-ing out the spirit of our scouts' maxim, " Never say die till you're dead," has risen to recovery and renewed health and strength.

It is equally possible for us as a nation, by energetically pluck-ing up spirit, recognizing our faults, and taking the proper rem-edies in time, not only to avoid becoming worse, but to rise to far greater power and to a potentiality for good in the world such as history has never seen.

And it is perhaps a more healthy sign if this should be done by the effort of the nation itself from within, than by the mere legislation of a statesman or two in its behalf.

WHERE AND HOW TO APPLY THE REMEDY

The evil is patent enough. The canker is there, yet little seems to be done officially beyond dressing the sore with sums of money. No steps are being taken to prevent its spreading deeper into our national life.

The natural field for any remedy lies in the rising generation and its upbringing.

Theodore Roosevelt, the ex-President of the United States of America, truly says :—

" If you are going to do anything permanent for the average man you have got to begin before he is a man. The chance of success lies in working with the boy, not with the man."

John Wanamaker says :—

" Save a man, you save one person; save a boy and you save a whole multiplication table."

The boys of the nation are full of enthusiasm and spirit, and only want their heads to be turned the right way to become good, useful citizens. This splendid material is being allowed to run to waste—nay, worse than that, it is allowed to become harmful to the nation simply for want of education, for want of a hand to guide them at the crisis of their lives when they are at the crossroads where their futures branch off for good or for evil.

They in their turn are to become the fathers of more boys, whom they are supposed to train up on right lines for good citizenship, when in reality they do not themselves know the haziest meaning of the word. This is not entirely their fault.

The present authorized scheme of education in our schools includes plenty of bookwork, but no development of the quality that counts, namely, *character*, which, after all, is of the first importance. Not thousands, but hundreds of thousands of boys in our great cities, after an education in reading sufficient to enable them to devour the horrors of the *Police News,* and in arithmetic to help them to make their football wagers, are being left to drift into the ranks of the " hooligans " and " wasters " without any attempt to stay them. But they receive no teaching in resourcefulness, chivalry, thrift, citizenship, or patriotism.

(*a*) How is it possible to apply a remedy for this?

(*b*) What form can the remedy take?

(*c*) How can a private individual help?

It is useless to attempt much with the present adult wasters.

(*a*) The remedy must be applied to the rising generation.

(*b*) Its aim should be to instil " character " into the men of the future.   By " character " is meant a spirit of manly self-reliance and of unselfishness—something of the *practical* Christianity which (although they are Buddhists in theory) distinguishes the Burmese in their daily life.

(*c*) Where the individual citizen can help in this great national work is shown by what has already been accomplished in this direction by the Boys' Brigade, Young Men's Christian Association, Church Lads' Brigade, and other numerous societies of the same kind.   Yet good as their work has been, with all their effort they only till a portion of the field.   They hold some 270,000 boys: but what is that out of the three and a half millions who need their help?

That they do not influence a greater number is due to:—

Want of amalgamation and mutual coöperation among the different societies.

Difficulty in getting enough young men to take up the work of training the boys.

Difficulty of attracting the boys and of maintaining their interest after they have got them.

ONE REMEDY AND ITS POSSIBILITIES

These deficiencies seemed to be remediable in some particulars, and induced me to suggest the scheme of " Scouting for Boys " as a step to meeting them, since being applicable to all these societies it might, by its common adoption, form a bond between them; by reason of its practical and sporting tendency and absence of red tape it might appeal to a wider field of possible instructors; and, above all, by its variety of attractions it would appeal directly to the boys themselves—even to the worst, the " hooligans."

" Boys is like pups," says the old Scout Rocky in " Jock of the Bushveldt "; " Boys is like pups—you've got to help 'em some, but not too much and not too soon. They've got to learn themselves. I reckon if a man's never made a mistake he's never had a good lesson. Mistakes is a part of the price of knowledge, but it's the part you don't like paying. That's why you remember it. Don't save a boy from making his mistakes. He don't know anything properly because he don't think; and he don't think because you saved him the trouble and he never knew how. No! S——! If he's got ter swim, you let him know right there thet the water's deep and ther ain't no one to hold him up, and if he don't wade in and larn, it's goin' to be his funeral."

The key to successful education is not so much to *teach* the pupil as to get him to *learn* for himself. The subject to be instilled must be made to appeal—you must lure your fish with a succulent worm, not with a bit of hard dry biscuit. Moreover, as Sir Clifford Allbut lately said to the Association of Science Masters of Public Schools:—

" The British boy, generally speaking, is a very matter-of-fact little person, very serious, very anxious, and very handy. Do we make his seriousness ours, or do we drive him out to his games? Do we attend to his ' How ' and ' Why,' or do we tell him that boys should not ask too many questions? "

That was my object in suggesting the gilt of " Scouting " for the pill of education in manliness or good citizenship; but I had no idea when I did so a year ago that it would meet with the response which it has done. Its intention has been recognized. It has been adopted by all the best associations for boys and by a large number of schools. It is also used on more than one of His Majesty's ships and in several units in the Army.

But a further result which had not been foreseen—at any rate, on a large scale—has been its rapid and widespread development as a separate organization of its own. This, although I had to some extent provided for it, I had not desired, as I believe in amalgamation and concentration of all such efforts for tackling the question with greater weight. But apparently the details of the system have commended themselves to the boys to the extent of their taking it up for themselves and of their looking round for officers to command them, which is rather the reverse of the usual procedure. And officers are more readily found because the scheme is elastic and leaves much to their own initiative and responsibility, without demanding a too rigid obedience to rules or the continual rendering of returns on their part.

Scouting has, therefore, broken out as a separate institution of its own, not only in most of our big towns in Great Britain and Ireland, but also in Australia, New Zealand, South Africa, Canada, with a promise of further extension in other countries such as Germany, America, Russia, Denmark, Norway, Austria, Argentina, and Chile.

THE GREAT POSSIBILITY

The suggestion has been made that since it has thus "caught on" with the boys themselves it might with proper organization form an instrument for instruction of every boy in the country.

Whether it does so or not depends entirely on our getting men to come forward to act as scoutmasters in every district, with that aim constantly before them, namely, of roping in everything in the shape of a boy that is not already under some influence for good.

HOW TO CATCH OUR BOYS

I do not in these "Hints" propose to teach my grandmother to suck eggs; and, therefore, I only address them to those who have had no previous practice in teaching boys, or who wish for explanations with which to meet criticisms or inquiries into our scheme. They are merely a few notes from my own small experience in that line, and tend to explain some of the arrangements of details in the Handbook.

When you are trying to get boys to come under good influence I have likened you to a fisherman wishful to catch fish.

If you bait your hook with the kind of food that you like yourself it is probable that you will not catch many—certainly not the shy, game kind of fish. You therefore use as bait the food that the fish likes.

So with boys; if you try to preach to them what you consider elevating matter you won't catch them. Any obvious "goody-goody" will scare away the more spirited among them, and those are the ones you want to get hold of. The only way is to hold out something that really attracts and interests them. And I think you will find that scouting does this.

You can afterwards season it with what you want them to have.

To get a hold on your boys you must be their *friend;* but don't be in too great a hurry at first to gain this footing until they have got over their shyness of you. Mr. F. D. How, in his "Book of the Child," sums up the right course in the following story :—

"A man whose daily walk led him down a certain dingy street saw a tiny boy with grimy face and badly-developed limbs playing with a banana-skin in the gutter. The man nodded to him—the boy shrank away in terror. Next day the man nodded again. The boy had decided there was nothing to be afraid of, and spat at the man. Next day the little fellow only stared. The day after he shouted " Hi! " as the man went on. In time the little fellow smiled back at the greeting which he now began to expect. Finally the triumph was complete when the boy—a tiny chap—was waiting at the corner and seized the man's fingers in his dirty little fist. It was a dismal street, but it became one of the very brightest spots in all that man's life."

" BE PREPARED "

In the Handbook I suggest as subjects to teach your boys such things as Observation of Details, and consequently ability to read character, and thereby to gain sympathy ; the value of patience and cheery good temper; the duty of giving up some of one's time and pleasure for helping one's country and fellow-men ; and the inner meaning of our motto, " Be Prepared."

But as you come to teach these things you will very soon find (unless you are a ready-made angel) that you are acquiring them yourself all the time.

You must " Be Prepared " yourself for disappointments at

first, though you will as often as not find them outweighed by
unexpected successes.

You must from the first "Be Prepared" for the prevailing
want of concentration of mind on the part of boys, and if you
then frame your teaching accordingly, I think you will have very
few disappointments.   Do not expect boys to pay great attention
to any one subject for very long until you have educated them
to do so.   You must meet them halfway, and not give them
too long a dose of one drink.   A short, pleasing sip of one
kind, and then off to another, gradually lengthening the sips till
they become steady draughts.

Thus a formal lecture on the subject which you want to
practise very soon palls on them, their thoughts begin to wander,
and they get bored because they have not learnt the art of
switching their mind where they want it to be, and *holding it
there.*

This making the mind amenable to the will is one of the
important inner points in our training.

For this reason it is well to think out beforehand each day
what you want to say on your subject, and then bring it out a
bit at a time as opportunity offers—at the camp-fire, or in intervals
of play and practice, not in one long set address.

You will find the lectures in the Handbook broken up into
sections for this purpose.

Frequent practical demonstrations and practices should be
sandwiched in between the sections of the lectures to hold the
attention of the boys and to drive home your theory.

THE IMPORTANCE OF A CLUBROOM

Half the battle is to get a room lent for certain nights in the
week, or hired as a club for the scouts, even if they only consist
of a patrol in the village.

It must be well lit and well ventilated to prevent depression
and boredom.   Pictures of incidents (not landscapes or old
portraits) help to make attraction.

A *bright* fire in winter.

Interesting illustrated books and magazines.

This can generally be got, furniture, games, etc., being given in the first instance by well-wishers.

A coffee-bar, commencing on the smallest lines, will generally succeed, and if carefully managed may develop a regular income for the upkeep of the clubroom.

The scouts themselves must do the cleaning and decorating, and making furniture.

Discipline and good order should be kept inside the room and neatness insisted on, patrol leaders being made responsible, patrols taking it in turn to be responsible for cleanliness and good order of the room for a week at a time.

If a bit of ground, even waste ground or a backyard, is available as a club ground, so much the better. You want some place where the scouts can make huts, light fires, play basketball, make tracks, etc.

Make the boys themselves manage the club affairs as far as possible. Sit back yourself and let them make their mistakes at first, till they can learn sense and responsibility.

In America small self-managed boys' clubs are becoming exceedingly numerous and popular in all towns and villages. And the education authorities help them by allowing them the use of classrooms in the school buildings in the evenings.

At the same time, when you can get your own clubroom, no matter how small, it gives the boys more of a sense of proprietorship and responsibility, especially if they have taken a hand themselves in making the furniture, putting up pictures, etc.

The clubroom must not be made cosey like a lady's boudoir, as the boys must be able to romp in it occasionally, or play handball, or " Bang the bear," etc. So you want furniture that will pack away into a corner, such as folding wooden chairs, small tables, and a cupboard in which to put away books, games, etc., when the romp comes on.

The ideal club is one of two rooms—one for quiet games, reading, and talking; the other for romping, gymnastics, etc.

The boys must, of course, pay a subscription towards rent, lighting, furnishing, etc., and the major expenses must be provided for by means of some joint work by them, such as garden produce, toys, displays, or a bazaar. One penny weekly, paid

strictly in advance, is usually sufficient as membership subscription.

A Penny Savings Bank should be started to enable boys to
put by money wherewith to pay for outings, and eventually to
start them in the practice of thrift.

I even advocate taking the boys to the theatre to see something really good—as a very great inducement to them to save
the money necessary to pay for their seats, and thus a first step
in thrift.

PLAYS

Boys are full of romance, and they love " make-believe " to a
greater extent than they like to show.

All you have to do is to play up to this, and to give rein
to your imagination to meet their requirements. But you have
to treat with all seriousness the many tickling incidents that
will arise; the moment you laugh at a situation the boys are
quick to feel that it is all a farce and to lose faith in it forth-
with and forever.

For instance, in instructing a patrol to make the call of its
tutelary animal, the situation borders on the ridiculous, but if
the instructor remains perfectly serious the boys work at it with
the idea that it is " business "—and, once accomplished, the
call becomes a fetish for *esprit de corps* among the members of
the patrol.

To stand on the right footing for getting the best out of
your boys you must see things with their eyes. To you the
orchard must, as it is with them, be Sherwood Forest with
Robin Hood and his Merry Men in the background; the fishing
harbor must be the Spanish Main with its pirates and privateers;
even the town common may be a prairie teeming with buffaloes
and Red Indians, or the narrow slum a mountain gorge where
live the bandits or the bears.

(Read the " Golden Age," by Kenneth Graham, and " Two
Little Savages," by E. T. Seton.)

Once you take this line you see how deadly dreary and how
wasteful seems the dull routine of drill upon which the unimaginative scoutmaster falls back for his medium of instruction.

Think out the points you want your boys to learn, and then make up games to bring them into practice.

Bacon said that play-acting was one of the best means of educating children, and one can quite believe him.

It develops the natural power in them of imitation, and of wit and imagination, all of which help in the development of character; and at the same time lessons of history and morality can be impressed on their minds far better by their assuming the characters and acting the incidents themselves than by any amount of preaching of the same on the part of the teacher.

The recent craze for historical pageants is in reality one of the best ideas educationally that have come over us of late years. In places where pageants have been held, both old and young have learnt—and learnt for the rest of their lives—something of the history of their forefathers, their town, and their country.

Instructors will find it a genuinely useful practice to make their scouts act scenes from history or incidents with which they desire to impress them. Such, for instance, as " Wilson's Last Stand," " The Wreck of the Birkenhead," " The Sentry at Pompeii."

When the performances attain a certain degree of merit, they might be used as a means of obtaining funds.

RESPONSIBILITY TO BOYS

The great thing in this scheme is to delegate responsibility—mainly through the patrol leaders.

Have, if possible, a good second in command to yourself to insure continuity of instruction should you be unable on occasions to present yourself, and to relieve you of many minor details of administration.

Give full responsibility and show full confidence in your patrol leaders. Expect a great deal from them and you will get it.

This is the key to success in scout-training.

Foster the patrol spirit and friendly rivalry between patrols, and you will get immediate good results in an improved standard of the whole. Don't try and do everything yourself, or the boys will merely look on, and the scheme will flag.

DISCIPLINE

Insist on discipline, and strict, quick obedience in small details; let them run riot only when you give leave for it, which is a good thing to do every now and then.

A nation to be powerful and prosperous must be well disciplined, and you only get discipline in the mass by discipline in the individual.   By discipline I mean patient obedience to authority and to other dictates of duty.

This cannot be got by repressive measures, but by encouragement and by educating the boy first in self-discipline and in sacrificing of self and selfish pleasures for the benefit of others. This teaching is largely effected by means of example, and by expecting it of him.   There lies our work.

Sir Henry Knyvett, in 1596, warned Queen Elizabeth that the State which neglects to train and discipline its youth produces not merely rotten soldiers or sailors, but the far greater evil of equally rotten citizens for civil life; or, as he words it, " For want of true discipline the honor and wealth both of Prince and countrie is desperatlie and frivolouslie ruinated."

Discipline is not gained by punishing a child for a bad habit, but by substituting a better occupation, that will absorb his attention, and gradually lead him to forget and abandon the old one.

CONTINENCE

In this Handbook I have touched upon many important items of a boy's education, but there is scarcely one more important than that of continence.

The training of the boy would be very incomplete did it not contain some clear explanation and plain-spoken instruction on this head.

The prudish mystery with which we have come to veil this important question among the youth of both sexes is doing incalculable harm.   The very secrecy with which we withhold all knowledge from the boy prompts him the more to take his own line equally secretly, and, therefore, injuriously.

I have never known a boy who was not the better for having
the matter put to him frankly and fully.   For an instructor to let
his boys walk on this exceedingly thin ice without giving them a
warning word, owing to some prudish sentimentality, would be
little short of a crime.

Every one should read " From Youth into Manhood," by
Winfield S. Hall, M. D. ; sexual hygiene for young men and older
boys. (50c.)   " Sex Instruction for Boys," Westminster Press,
Philadelphia. (2c.)

SEA SCOUTING

Sea scouting has been introduced into this edition because it
may be of value to the country and to numbers of our boys.

In *The Nautical Magazine* it was recently shown that in the
last fifteen years the Mercantile Marine, which should be the
mainstay of British commerce and a backing to the Royal Navy
in case of war, has increased by 26,000 men.   Of these, 15,000
were colored men, 11,000 foreigners, 810 British.

Yet we have crowds of men in Britain wanting work, while
foreigners man our ships.

The call of the sea is not sounded in the ears of our boys as it
used to be.

In many places it is possible to get the use of boats and hulks,
instead of going into camp, where seamanship can be taught with
all its good points of handiness, resourcefulness, activity, and
health.

THRIFT

A very large proportion of the distress and unemployedness in
our country is directly due to the want of thrift on the part of the
people themselves.   Our social reformers, before seeking for new
remedies, would do well to set this part of the problem right in
the first place.   They would then probably find very little more
left for them to do.   There is money enough to go round
if it were properly made use of by all workingmen.   In
many places, where thrift is practised, the men save their pay,

buy their own houses, and become prosperous and contented citizens in happy homes.   This might be very widely extended.

Mr. Will Crooks has himself pointed out that there is little hope of genuine relief to the workingman until he helps himself by realizing his duties as a citizen and as the head of his home, by seeing the folly of paying over his earnings to the bookmaker and the publican instead of to his wife and the bank.

While we deposit an average of four pounds per head in the Savings Bank, other nations put in much more, Denmark topping the list with nineteen pounds per head.   Our wastefulness is almost inconceivable and might well be made criminal.

If the rising generation could be started on a career of saving and thrift a great difference would result in the character and prosperity of the nation in the near future.   In Manchester the school children have been encouraged to save by means of money-boxes, and there are now 44,000 depositors in the Savings Banks.

For this reason we have instituted money-boxes for Boy Scouts.

OBJECTIONS TO SCOUTING

In your work of spreading our scheme you will, of course, meet with critics who will object to various points in it, such as: militarism, want of religious training, abuse of Sunday, want of drill, the absurdity of plays and war dances.

Most of these objections I have already dealt with, but I should like to say a few words on

MILITARISM

There is no military meaning attached to the name scouting. Peace scouting comprises the attributes of colonial frontiersmen in the way of resourcefulness and self-reliance and the many other qualities which make them men among men.   There is no intention of making the lads into soldiers or of teaching them bloodthirstiness. ᐟ But under patriotism they will be taught that a citizen must be prepared to take his fair share among his fellows in the defence of the homeland against aggression in return for the safety and freedom enjoyed by him as an inhabitant. He who leaves this duty to others to do for him is neither playing a plucky nor a fair part.

I have never met a man who has seen war in a civilized country who remained a so-called anti-militarist. He knows too well the awful and cruel results of war, and until nations have agreed to disarm he will not invite aggression or leave his country at the mercy of an enemy by neglecting its defence. You might just as well abolish the police in order to do away with crime before you have educated the masses not to steal.

DRILL

I am continually being asked by officers—not by the boys—to introduce more drill into the training of Boy Scouts; but although, after experience of thirty-four years of it, I recognize the disciplinary value of drill; I also see very clearly its evils. Briefly they are these:—

(1) Drill gives a feeble, unimaginative officer a something with which to occupy his boys. He does not consider whether it appeals to them or really does them good. It saves *him* a world of trouble.

(2) Drill tends to destroy individuality, and when once it has been learnt it bores a boy who is longing to be tearing about on some enterprise or other; it blunts his keenness.

RELIGION

An organization of this kind would fail in its object if it did not bring its members to a knowledge of religion—but the usual fault in such cases is the manner in which this is done. If it were treated more as a matter of everyday life and quite unsectarian it would not lose its dignity and it would gain a hold. The definition of religious observance is purposely left vague in this Handbook in order to give a free hand to organizations and units making use of it, so that they can give their own instructions in the matter. In our association dealing with Jews, Hindoos, Greek Church, as well as with Catholics and Protestants, we cannot lay down strict sectarian ideas—if we would. It is often the best to introduce it by " sips " here and there among other instruction, in every branch, as I suggest in the chapters on " Chivalry," Boy Exercises, and elsewhere in this book. This is a matter for the discretion of the scoutmaster.

Charles Stelzle, in his " Boys of the Streets and How to Win Them," says :—

" Sometimes we are so much concerned about there being enough religion in our plans for the boy, that we forget to leave enough boy in the plans. According to the notions of some, the ideal boys' club would consist of prayer meetings and Bible classes, with an occasional missionary talk as a treat and perhaps magic lantern views of the Holy Land as a dizzy climax."

Religion can and ought to be taught to the boy, but not in a milk-and-watery way, or in a mysterious and lugubrious manner ; he is very ready to receive it if it is shown in its heroic side and as a natural every-day quality in every proper man, and it can be well introduced to boys through the study of nature. The study of God's work is a fit subject for Sunday instruction. For this reason the scouting suggested for use on Sundays in a Christian country is—to attend Church or Church-parade, and then to devote the rest of the day to scouting, in the shape of Nature study. To watch the habits of animals, and to study the wonders of the plants or insect life and so on is better than that Sunday loafing which at present ruins a very large proportion of our young men—and girls. A number of Sunday schools have now taken up " Scouting " in this way as part of their training, and with best results. There is no need for this instruction to be dismal, that is, " all tears and texts." Arthur Benson, writing in " The Cornhill Magazine," says there are four Christian virtues, not three. They are Faith, Hope, Charity—and Humor. So also in the morning prayer of Robert Louis Stevenson :—

" The day returns and brings us the petty round of irritating concerns and duties. Help us to play the man—help us to perform them with laughter and kind faces. Let cheerfulness abound with industry. Give us to go blithely on our business all this day. Bring us to our resting beds weary and content and undishonored, and grant us in the end the gift of sleep."

TO SUM UP

The whole object of our scheme is to seize the boy's character in its red-hot stage of enthusiasm, and to weld it into the right shape and to encourage and develop its individuality—so that the boy may become a good man and a valuable citizen for our country in the immediate future, instead of being a waste of God's material.

The nation is showing signs of illness. We can diagnose it as "bad citizenship." We know the kind of remedy to apply, namely, education of the rising generation in "character."

"Scouting" offers one such remedy—if only as a "First Aid" pending the application of a better one. Meantime every minute is precious.

The remedy needs widespread application. This can be got if every scout is made to bring in a recruit before he receives his badge; and, especially, if every scout-officer and *every man or woman who reads this* will make an earnest effort to obtain a worker to take up the training, and in his turn to obtain the services of yet another.

It is by such a "snowball" movement that we may hope to take a really useful part in bringing strength, both moral and physical, to our ailing country.

BOOKS ON THE SUBJECT

"The Boy Problem." A study of boys and how to train them. By W. B. Forbush. (Progress Press, Boston, U. S. A.)

PART II. SIGNS AND SIGNALLING

SIGNALLING

Armies, scouts, and Indians use systems of signals which are the same in essentials, but varied to meet the means at hand.

Smoke-signals are universal. A bright fire is made, then smothered with green stuff, so that it sends up a column of thick smoke.

The ordinary use of smoke-fire signals is sufficiently set forth in the diagrams. Baden-Powell gives the following:—

"*Smoke-Signals:* Three big puffs in slow succession means " Go on." A succession of small puffs mean " Rally, come here." A continued column of smoke means " Halt." Alternate small puffs and big ones mean " Danger."

But it is possible to use a single column of smoke with the Morse code. Two men cover the smoky fire with a wet blanket, remove it, and let the smoke ascend for a second, for a dot. Then cover 4 seconds for space, and uncover for 3 seconds for a dash.

Or, at night, the same effect is obtained with a bright fire that is shown one second and two seconds for dot and dash, or screened four seconds for space.

But these and many other means of signalling presuppose a knowledge of the Morse code. This I shall give, first, as in the textbooks, and then, so as to convey it quickly, in a " remember-able " form, which any one can learn in an hour or so.

In the American Civil War Captain Clowry, a scout officer, wanted to give warning to a large force of his own army that the enemy were going to attack it unexpectedly during the night; but he could not get to his friends because there was a flooded river between them which he could not cross, and a storm of rain was going on.

What would you have done if you had been in his place?

54

A good idea struck him.   He got hold of an old railway engine that was standing near him.   He lit the fire and got up steam in her, and then started to blow the whistle with short and long blasts—what is called the Morse alphabet.   Soon his friends heard and understood, and answered back with a bugle.   And he then spelt out a message of warning to them, which they read and acted upon.   And so their force of 20,000 men was saved from surprise.

Lieutenant Boyd-Alexander describes in his book, " From the Niger to the Nile," how a certain tribe of natives in Central Africa signal news to each other by means of beats on a drum. And I have known tribes in the forests of the West Coast of Africa who do the same.

Every scout ought to learn the " dot and dash," or Morse method of signalling, because it comes in most useful whenever you want to send messages some distance by flag signalling, as in the Army and Navy, and it is also useful in getting you employment as a telegraphist.   It is not difficult to learn if you set about it with a will.   I found it most useful once during the Boer War. My column had been trying to get past a Boer force which was holding a pass in the mountains.   Finding they were too strong for us we gave it up late in the evening, and, leaving a lot of fires, alight, as if we were in camp in front of them, we moved during the night by a rapid march right round the end of the mountain range, and by daylight next day we were exactly in rear of them without their knowing it.   We then found a telegraph line, evidently leading from them to their headquarters some fifty miles farther off, so we sat down by the telegraph wire and attached our own little wire to it and read all the messages they were sending, and they gave us most valuable information.   But we should not have been able to do that had it not been that some of our scouts could read the Morse code.

Then the semaphore signalling, which is done by waving your arms at different angles to each other, is most useful and quite easy to learn, and is known by every soldier and sailor in the service.   Here you have all the different letters, and the different angles at which you have to put your arms to represent those letters; and though it looks complicated in the picture, when you come to work it out you will find it is very simple.

MORSE CODE

A	.−		N	−.
B	−...		O	−−−
C	−.−.		P	.−−.
D	−..		Q	−−.−
E	.		R	.−.
F	..−.		S	...
G	−−.		T	−
H	....		U	..−
I	..		V	...−
J	.−−−		W	.−−
K	−.−		X	−..−
L	.−..		Y	−.−−
M	−−		Z	−−..

Call signal		etc.	Erase		(A A A A A)
Answering		etc.	Go on		(G)
Spelling		(F F)	Wait		(M G)
Repeat		(I M I)	Right		(R T)
Full stop		(A A A)	Numeral		(F I)
Code flag		(M M)	Annul		(W W)

REMEMBERABLE MORSE

or Re-morse Alphabet

By this method it is possible to learn the Morse
alphabet in less than an hour

(All rights reserved)

WIG-WAG OR MYER CODE

From A. Duane's Rules for Signalling, 1901

Alphabet

A —	22	J — 1122		S —	212
B — 2112		K — 2121		T —	2
C —	121	L — 221		U —	112
D —	222	M — 1221		V — 1222	
E —	12	N —	11	W — 1121	
F — 2221		O —	21	X — 2122	
G — 2211		P — 1212		Y —	111
H —	122	Q — 1211		Z — 2222	
I —	1	R —	211	TION — 1112	

Official Conventional Signs

End of a word	3
End of a sentence	33
End of a message	333
I understand	22.22.3
Cease signalling	22.22.22.333
Repeat last word	121.121.3

TO SIGNAL WITH FLAG OR TORCH,—WIG-WAG

There are but *one* primary position and *three* motions.

The *primary position* is with the flag or other signal apparatus held vertically in front of the center of the body, butt of staff at height of waist, signalman facing squarely towards the station with which it is desired to communicate.

The *first motion,* or " one " or " 1," is a motion of the flag to the right of the sender. It should embrace an arc of 90°, starting at the vertical and returning to it without pause, and should be made in a plane exactly at right angles to the line connecting the two signal stations.

The *second motion,* or " two " or " 2," is a similar motion to the left of the sender.

To make the *third motion,* " front " or " three " or " 3," the flag is waved to the ground directly in front of the sender, and instantly returned to the vertical position.

Make a slight but distinct pause after each " letter," also after each " front."

REMEMBERABLE MYER

Two elements — a thick and a thin, *i. e.* **2** and **1**

A . 22 . Angry Apes

B . 2112 , Beauty

C . 121 . Cook & Candles

D . 222 . Drei Donkeys

E . 12 Emu & Elephant

F 2221 Funny Fruit

G . 2211 Girls & Goats

H . 122 Happy Hooligans

I . 1 . 1.

J . 1122 Jays & Jam

K . 2121 Kountry Kupples

L . 221 Lambs & Lady

M . 1221 Maps & Monkeys

N . 11 . Ninepins

O . 21 , Owl & Onion

P . 1212 , Pots & Paddles

Q . 1211 Queer Quirks

R . 211 Ram Race

S . 212 Soup & Sausage

T . 2 Tea Two

U . 112 Unicorn

V . 1222 Viper or Venison

W . 1121 Wonderful Windmill

X 2122 Xtreme Xpressions

Y . 111 Yoemen

Z 2222 Zoo Zoo Zoo Zoo or Two Two Two Two

THE SEMAPHORE SIGNAL CODE

May be done with semaphore, flags, or merely one's arms

This row is a circle with one flag or arm.

This row is a circle with two flags, one fixed at 45° to right.

This row is a circle with two flags, one fixed level to right.

Full stop.............. A A A
Right .... R T
Repeat................. I M I
Very end of Message.. V E

Words in parenthesis .... K K
Words underlined............ L L
Words in inverted commas.... R R
Message read......... ...... R D

INDIAN SIGNS AND BLAZES

Shaking a blanket, I want to talk to you.
Hold up a tree-branch, I want to make peace.
Hold up a weapon, means war; I am ready to fight.
Hold up a pole horizontally, with hands on it, I have found something.

(A later issue will give 100 principal signs of the Indian Sign-Language.)

 This is good water.

 Good water not far in this direction.

 A long way to good water, go in direction of arrow.

 Peace.

 War or trouble about.

 We camped here because one of us was sick.

 Road to be followed.

 Letter hidden three paces from here in the direction of the arrow.

 This path not to be followed.

 "I have gone home."

See "Rules for Signalling on Land and Sea," by Alexander Duane. N.Y., 1901.

How to climb a tree that is too thick.—Fell
a small tree against it.

THE WATCH AS A COMPASS

The watch is often used to give the compass-point exactly. Thus: Point the hour hand to the sun, then, in the morning, halfway between the hour hand and noon is due south. If afternoon, one must reckon halfway backward.

Thus, at 8 A. M., point the hour hand to the sun and reckon *back* halfway; the south is at 10. If at 4 P. M., point the hour hand at the sun and reckon back halfway. The south is at 2 o'clock.

The "halfway" is because the sun makes a course of twenty-four hours and the clock of but twelve. If we had a rational time-piece of twenty-four hours, it would fit in much better with all nature, and with the hour-hand pointed to the sun would make 12 o'clock, noon, always south.

If you cannot see the sun, get into a clear, open space, hold your knife-point upright on your watch-dial, and it will cast a faint shadow, showing where the sun really is, unless the clouds are very heavy.

OLD SAYINGS AND WEATHER SIGNS

When the dew is on the grass,
Rain will never come to pass.

When the grass is dry at night,
Look for rain before the light.
When grass is dry at morning light,
Look for rain before the night.

Three days' rain will empty any sky.

A deep, clear sky of fleckless blue
Breeds storms within a day or two.

When the wind is in the east,
It's good for neither man nor beast.

When the wind is in the north,
The old folk should not venture forth.
When the wind is in the south,
It blows the bait in the fishes' mouth.
When the wind is in the west,
It is of all the winds the best.

An opening and a shetting
Is a sure sign of a wetting.

(Another version)
Open and shet,
Sure sign of wet.

(Still another)
It's lighting up to see to rain.

Evening red and morning gray
Sends the traveller on his way.
Evening gray and morning red
Sends the traveller home to bed.

Red sky at morning, the shepherd takes warning;
Red sky at night is the shepherd's delight.

If the sun goes down cloudy Friday, sure of a clear Sunday.

If the rooster crows standing on fence or high place, it will clear;
If on the ground, it doesn't count.

Between eleven and two
You can tell what the weather is going to do.

Rain before seven, clear before eleven.

Fog in the morning, bright sunny day.
If it rains, and the sun is shining at the same time, the devil is whipping his wife and it will surely rain to-morrow.
If it clears off during the night, it will rain shortly again.
Sun drawing water, sure sign of rain.
A circle round the moon means " storm." As many stars as are in circle, so many days before it will rain.

Sudden heat brings thunder.

A storm that comes against the wind is always a thunderstorm.

The oak and the ash draw lightning. Under the birch and balsam you are safe.

East wind brings rain.

West wind brings clear, bright, cool weather.

North wind brings cold.

South wind brings heat. (On Atlantic coast.)

The rain-crow or cuckoo (both species) is supposed by all hunters to foretell rain, when its " Kow, kow, kow " is long and hard.

So, also, the tree-frog cries before rain.

Swallows flying low is a sign of rain; high, of clearing weather.

OUTDOOR PROVERBS

What weighs an ounce in the morning, weighs a pound at night.

A pint is a pound the whole world round.

Allah reckons not against a man's allotted time the days he spends in the chase.

If there's only one, it isn't a track, it's an accident.

Better safe than sorry.

No smoke without fire.

The bluejay doesn't scream without reason.

The worm don't see nuffin pretty 'bout de robin's song.—(Darkey.)

Ducks flying overhead in the woods are generally pointed for water.

If the turtles on a log are dry, they have been there half an hour or more, which means no one has been near to alarm them.

Cobwebs across a hole mean nothing inside.

MEASURING DISTANCES

(See " Two Little Savages," 1903)

The height of a tree is easily measured when on a level, open place, by measuring the length of its shadow, then comparing that with your own shadow, or that of a 10-foot pole.

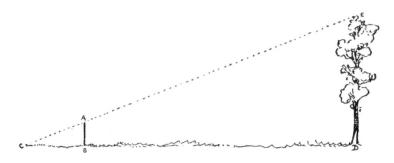

Thus, the 10-foot pole is casting a 15-foot shadow, and the tree's shadow is 150 feet long. apply the simple rule of three:

$$15 : 150 :: 10 : x = 100$$

But it is seldom so easy, and the good old rule of the triangle can be safely counted on: Get a hundred or more feet from your tree, on open ground, as nearly as possible on the level of its base. Set up a 10-foot pole (AB). Then mark the spot where the exact line from the top of the tree over the top of the pole touches the ground (C). Now, measure the distance from that spot (C) to the foot of the 10-foot pole (B); suppose it is 20 feet. Measure also the distance from that spot (C) to the base of the tree (D); suppose it is 120 feet, then your problem is:

$$20 : 10 :: 120 : x = 60$$

i.e., if at that angle 20 feet from the eye gives 10 feet elevation, 120 feet must give 60.

To make a right angle, make a triangle whose sides are exactly 6, 8, and 10 feet or inches each (or multiples of these). The angle opposite the 10 must be a true right-angle.

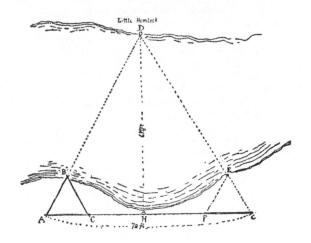

There are many ways of measuring distance across rivers, etc., without crossing. The simplest, perhaps, is by the equilateral triangle. Cut three poles of exactly equal length; peg them together into a triangle. Lay this on the bank of the river so one side points to some point on the opposite bank. Drive in three pegs to mark the exact points of this triangle (A,B,C). Then move it along the bank until you find a place (F,E,G) where its base is on line with the two pegs, where the base used to be, and one side in line with the point across the river (D). The width of the river is seven-eighths of the base of this great triangle.

Another method is by the isosceles triangle. Make a right-angied triangle as above, with sides 6, 8, and 10 feet (A,B,C); then, after firmly fixing the right-angle, cut down the 8-foot side to 6 feet, and saw off the 10-foot side to fit. Place this with the side *D B* on the river bank in line with the sight object (X) across. Put three pegs to mark the three corner places. Then take the triangle along the bank in the direction of *C* until *C' D'* are in line with the sight object, while B' C' is in line with the pegs b c. Then the length of the long base BC^1 will equal the distance from B to X.

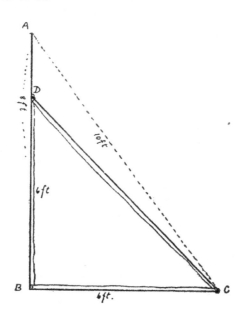

To make a right angle

To measure the space between two distant objects, D and E. Line A B on one, then move this right-angled triangle until F G is lined on the other, with B G in line with G H. B G equals the space between D and E then.

If the distance is considerable, it may be measured sometimes by sound. Thus, when a gun is fired, a man is chopping, or a dog barking, count the seconds between the sight and the sound of the blow and multiply by 1,100 feet, which is the distance sound travels in a second.

Occasionally, the distance of an upright bank, cliff, or building can be measured by the echo. Half the seconds between shout and echo, multiplied by 1,100, gives the distance in feet.

The usual way to estimate long distances is by the time they take to cover.   Thus, a good canoe on dead water goes 4 to 5

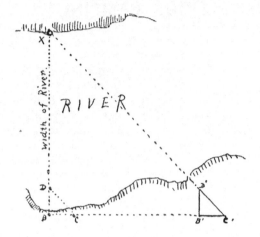

miles an hour.   A man afoot walks 3½ miles an hour on good roads.   A packtrain goes 2½ miles an hour, or perhaps only 1½ on the mountain trails.

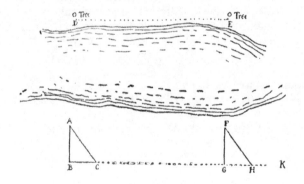

A man's thumb is an inch wide.
Span of thumb and longest finger, 9 inches.
Brisk walking pace is 1 yard.

PART III. CAMPING

CAMPING TRIPS

As a rule, it is better to go on a trip with a definite object. If you go with a general vague determination to get healthy, you are likely to think too much about it. It is better to live correctly, and safely assume that you will be healthier for the trip. To illustrate: One of my trips was made to determine the existence of Wood Buffalo on the Great Slave River; another to prove that the Canadian Fauna reached the Lake of the Woods. Some of my friends have made trips to win the badge of expert canoe-man; others for the camper badge, and so forth.

Many mothers ask with fear, " Won't my boy catch cold, if he camps out?" This is the last and least of dangers. Almost never does one catch cold in camp. I have found it much more likely that boys suffer through irregular hours of eating and sleeping; but these are troubles that the camp discipline is designed to meet.

There is one great evil that campers should beware of, that is rheumatism. But none need suffer if they will take the simple precaution of changing their wet clothes when not in action, and never sleeping directly on the ground. A warm, dry place for the bed should be prepared in every tent and teepee.

Good books to have with you:

" Camp Kits and Camp Life," by Charles Stedman Hauks (Scribner's, 1906).

" The Book of Camping and Woodcraft," by Horace Kephart (*Outing*, 1908).

" Emergencies," by Charlotte Vetter Gulick (Ginn & Co., 1909).

" The Frontiersman's Pocketbook," by Roger Pocock (Murray, 1909).

" The Boy Pioneers," by Dan C. Beard (Scribner's, 1909).

" A Woman Tenderfoot," by Grace G. Seton (Doubleday).

71

OUTFIT FOR A PARTY OF SIX CAMPING ONE WEEK
(FIXED CAMP)

1 12-foot teepee (if for cold weather), accommodating five or six men. Or, in summer, a

10 x 12 wall tent.

1 8 x 10 awning for kitchen and dining-room, in hot or wet weather.

5 yards mosquito-bar and some dope.

3 or 4 one-gallon bags of cotton for supplies.

A few medicines and pill-kit or " first aid," including cold cream for sunburn.

1 strong clothes-line; ball of cord; ball of twine; ball of strong linen pack-thread.

Axe.

A sharp hatchet.

Claw-hammer.

Whetstone.

Small crosscut saw.

Spade.

File.

Packing needles and sewing-kit for repairing clothes.

Nails: One lb. of 1½, two lbs. of 2½, two lbs. of 3½, and one lb. of 5-inch.

Pocket tool outfit (A, K, and B is good).

Soap.

Mirror.

Toilet-paper.

Waterproof match-box.

A locker.

Cooking outfit: Either a ready-made, self-nesting " Buzza-cot," or

3 cover-kettles, 10-qt., 4-qt., and 2-qt. (riveted, not soldered).

2 frying-pans, with handles and covers.

2 big spoons.

Coffee strainer.

1 Dutch oven.

1 wire grill.
2 bake-pans.
1 butcher knife.
Salt and pepper casters.
Tin boxes to hold stock of same.
2 folding buckets.
2 folding wash-basins.
Dishpan.
Tea-pot (riveted).
Coffee-pot (riveted).
Dish-cloths and towels.
Soap.
Folding lantern and supply of candles.
4 flat steel rods to cook on.
And for each man, plate, cup, saucer, and porringer (preferably enamelled); also knife, fork, and spoon.
And such other things as are dictated by previous experience, or for use in the games to be played.

Besides which each member has his ordinary clothes, with a change, and toilet-bag, also:
A rubber blanket.
2 wool blankets.
1 cotton or burlap bed-tick, 2½ x 6¼ ft.
Swimming-trunks.
A pair of brown sneaks.
A war-sack of waterproof.
Khaki suit.
Fishing-tackle and guns, according to choice.
Pocket-knife.

(D. T. Abercrombie & Co., 311 Broadway, or Abercrombie & Fitch, 57 Reade Street, New York, for all supplies.)

Food to last six fellows one week:
Oatmeal .... 6 lbs.
Rice .... 2 lbs.
Crackers ....20 lbs.
Chocolate .... 1 lb.

Tea ....½ lb.
Coffee .... 3 lbs.
Lard .... 5 lbs.
Sugar .... 6 lbs.
Condensed milk .... 6 tins
Butter .... 3 lbs.
Eggs .... 3 dozen
Bacon ....15 lbs.
Preserves .... 5 lbs.
Prunes .... 3 lbs.
Maple syrup .... 3 quarts
Cheese .... 1 lb.
Raisins .... 3 lbs.
Potatoes ....½ bushel
White beans .... 3 quarts
Canned corn .... 3 tins
Flour ....25 lbs.
Baking-powder .... 1 lb.
Concentrated soups ....½ lb.
Salt .... 2 lbs.
Pepper .... 1 ounce

Fresh fish and game are pleasant variations, but seem to make little difference in the grocery bill.

TENTS

There are many styles of small tents on the market; almost any of them answer very well. For those who wish to equip themselves with the latest and best, a 10 x 12-foot wall tent of 10-ounce double-filled army duck, stained or dyed yellow, brown, or dull green, is best. It will accommodate a party of five or six.

For tramping trips, light tents of waterproof silk are made. One large enough for a man weighs only two or three lbs.

Any of the established makers can supply what is needed, if they know the size of the party and nature of the outing.

TEEPEE

The Indian teepee has the great advantage of ventilation and an open fire inside. It has the disadvantage of needing a lot of poles and of admitting some rain by the smoke-hole. It will be fully described later.

NEW STYLE TEEPEE

A new style of teepee, invented by myself some years ago, has been quite successful, since it combines the advantages of teepee

and tent and needs only four poles beside the smoke-poles. It is, however, less picturesque than the old style.

This can be got at D. T. Abercrombie & Co., 311 Broadway, New York.

This gives the great advantage of an open fire inside, and good ventilation, while it is quite rainproof.

CAMP-GROUNDS

In selecting a good camp-ground, the first thing is a dry, level place near good *wood* and good *water*. If you have horses or oxen, you must also have grass.

Almost all Indian camps face the east, and, when ideal, have some storm-break or shelter on the west and north. Then, they get the morning sun and the afternoon shade in summer, and in winter avoid the coldest winds and drifting snows, which in most of the country east of the Rockies come from the north and west.

Sometimes local conditions make a different exposure desirable, but not often. For obvious reasons, it is well to be near one's boat-landing.

After pitching the tent or teepee, dig a trench around, with a drain on the low side to prevent flooding.

Each small camp, or group of tents in a large camp, has a sanitary ditch or hole. There is a narrow trench a foot wide, surrounded by a screen of bushes or canvas. It is made narrow enough to straddle. Each time after use, a shovelful of dry earth is thrown in.

All camps must be left as clear of filth, scraps, papers, tins, bottles, etc., as though a human being had never been there.

BEDS

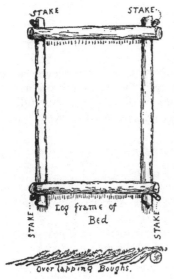

Log frame of Bed

Overlapping Boughs.

Every dealer in camp-outfits can produce an array of different camp-beds, cots, and sleeping-bags, that shows how important it is to be dry and warm when you sleep.

The simplest plan is the oldest one, two pair of blankets and a waterproof under-sheet on a neatly laid bed of evergreen boughs, dry leaves, or dry grass. The ideal way of laying the boughs is shown in the figure.

Sleeping-bags I gave up long ago. They are too difficult to air, or to adjust to different temperatures.

Rubber beds are luxurious, but heavy for a pack-outfit, and in cold weather they need thick blankets over them, otherwise they are too cool.

Old campers generally agree that there is nothing finer than a " bed boughed down with care."

LIGHTS

For camp use, there is nothing better than the Stonebridge folding-lantern, with a good supply of candles.

But a temporary torch can readily be made of pine knots or roots in a split stick of green wood, and a fairly steady light can be made of a piece of cotton cloth or twisted rag stuck in a clam-shell full of melted grease or oil. An improvement on the last is easily made by putting the cotton wick on a stick, which is, by help of a base of wet clay, able to stand upright in the grease. Another improvement is made by using a tin in place of the shell. It makes a steadier lamp, as well as a much larger light.

This kind of lamp has wide use and some queer names.

WATER

If there is swamp or pond, but no pure water at hand, you can dig an Indian well in half an hour. This is simply a hole about 18 inches across and down about 6 inches below water-level, a few paces from the pond. Bail it out quickly; let it fill again; bail it a second time, and the third time it fills, it will be full of filtered water, clear of everything except matter actually dissolved.

MOSQUITOES, BLACK FLIES, ETC.

If you are camping in mosquito or fly season, the trip may be ruined, if you are not fully prepared.

For extreme cases, use the ready-made head-nets. They are hot, but effectual. You can easily get used to the net; no man can stand the flies. In my Arctic trip of 1907, we could not have endured life without the nets. Indians and all wore them.

Of the various dopes that are used, one of the simplest and best is Colonel N. Fletcher's, given in Kephart's "Book of Camping and Woodcraft":

" Pure pine tar ....1 oz.
Oil pennyroyal ....1 oz.
Vaseline ....3 ozs.

Mix cold in a mortar. If you wish, you can add 3 per cent. carbolic acid to above. Some make it 1½ ozs. tar."

In certain crowded camps there is danger of headlice and body vermin. I have heard washing in potato water recommended as a sure cure. Potato water is the water potatoes have been boiled in. Most drugshops have tobacco ointment and blue ointment; a very little of these applied to the body where there is hair is a sure cure.

CAMP ROUTINE

6.30 A.M.	Turn out, bathe, etc.
7.00	Breakfast.
8.00	Air bedding in sun, if possible.
9.00	Scouting games and practice.
11.00	Swimming.
12.00 M.	Dinner.
1.00 P.M.	Talk by leader.
2.00	Water games, etc.
6.00	Supper.
7.30	Evening council around camp-fire. Order of business:

Opening council.
Roll-call.
Record of last council.
Reports of scouts.
Left-over business.
Complaints.
Honors.
New scouts.
New business.
Challenges.
Social doings, songs, dances, stories.
Closing council (devotional services when desired).

10.00	Lights out.

CAMP-FIRES

The day Columbus landed (probably) the natives remarked: " White man fool, make big fire, can't go near; Indian make little fire and sit happy."

Now we all know that a camp without a camp-fire would be no camp at all; its chiefest charm would be absent.

Your first care, then, is to provide for a small fire and prevent it spreading. In the autumn this may mean very elaborate clearing, or burning, or wetting of a space around the fire. In the winter it means nothing.

Cracked Jimmy, in " Two Little Savages," gives very practical directions for lighting a fire anywhere in the timbered northern part of America: thus,

" First a curl of birch-bark as dry as it can be,
Then some twigs of soft wood, dead, but on the tree,
Last of all some pine-knots to make the kittle foam,
And there's a fire to make you think you're settin' right at
    home."

If you have no birch-bark, it is a good plan to shave a dry soft-wood stick, leaving all the shavings sticking on the end in

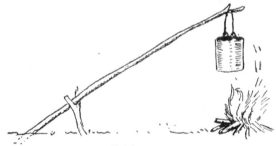

Pot-hanger

a fuzz, like a Hopi prayer stick. Several of these make a sure fire kindler. Fine splinters may be made quickly by hammering a small stick with the back of the axe.

And in the case of a small party and hasty camp, you need nothing but a pot-hanger of green wood for a complete kitchen, and many hundreds of times, on prairie and in forest, I found this sufficient.

A more elaborate camp kitchen is made of four green logs (aspen preferred), set 3 inches apart at one end, 10 at the other, with a fire on the ground and between, flattened on top and in the middle. The pots sit on the opening between the top logs. Sometimes stones of right size and shape are used instead of the logs, but the stones do not contribute anything to the heat and are less manageable.

In addition to this log-grate, more elaborate camps have a

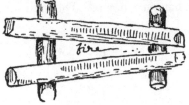

Green log grate

hanger as below, on which are pot-hooks of green wood.

In wet weather, an axeman can always get dry wood by cutting into a standing dead tree, or on the under side of down timber that is not entirely on the ground.

On the prairies and plains, since buffalo chips are no more, we use horse and cow chips, kindled with dry grass and roots of sage-brush, etc.

To keep a fire alive all night, bank the coals: *i.e.*, bury them in ashes.

Always put out the fire on leaving camp.
It is a crime to leave a burning fire.
Use buckets of water, if need be.

FIREARMS

No one under fourteen years of age should be allowed the use of a gun or pistol.

The didn't-know-it-was-loaded fool is the cause of more sorrow than the deliberate murderer.

For any scout to point a firearm at any one is a crime. If he didn't know it was loaded, he should be still more severely punished.

Never let the muzzle of the gun sweep the horizon.

Never carry a gun full-cock or hammer down. The half-cock is made for safety. Use it.

Never pull a gun by the muzzle.

Never shoot at anything about which you are in doubt.

CAMP COOKERY

(See Horace Kephart's " Book of Camping and Woodcraft ")

Can scarcely be separated from the camp-fire. In most camps the staples are: Coffee (or tea), bacon, game, fish and hardtack, bannocks or biscuit, usually and most appropriately called " sinkers " and " damper."

To make these necessary evils, take

1 pint flour.

1 teaspoonful of baking-powder.

Half as much salt.

Twice as much grease or lard.

With water enough to make into paste, say one-half a pint.

When worked into smooth dough, shape it into wafers, half an inch thick, and three inches across. Set in a greased tin, which is tilted up near a steady fire. Watch and turn the tin till all are browned evenly.

For other and better but more elaborate methods of making bread, see Kephart's book as above.

For cooking fish and game, the old, simple standbys are the frying-pan and the stew-pan.

As general rule, mix all batters, mush, etc., with cold water, and always cook with a slow fire.

There is an old adage:

> Hasty cooking is tasty cooking.
> Fried meat is dried meat.
> Boiled meat is spoiled meat.
> Roast meat is best meat.

This reflects perhaps the castle kitchen rather than the camp, but it has its measure of truth, and the reason why roast meat

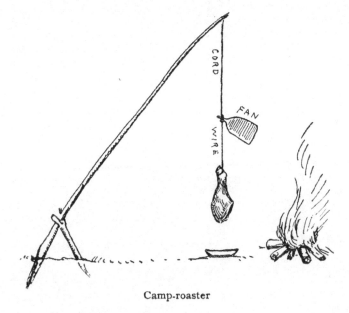

Camp-roaster

is not more popular is because it takes so much time and trouble to make it a success.

During my Barren Ground trip I hit on a remarkably successful roaster that, so far as I know, was never tried before.

The usual pot-stick is set in the ground (if no tree be near), and the roast hung by a wire and a cord; where they meet is a straight or flat piece of wood, or bark, set in a loop of the wire.

The wind strikes on this, causing the roast to turn; it goes till the cord is wound up; then unwinds itself and goes on unceasingly. We used it every day. It was positively uncanny to see the way in which this thing kept on winding and unwinding itself, all day long, if need be.

HOW TO MAKE A FIRE BY RUBBING STICKS

(By Ernest Thompson Seton)

(Copyrighted by *Country Life in America*, June, 1904)

" How do the Indians make a fire without matches? " asked a boy who loved to " play Indian." Most of us have heard the answer to this—" the Indians use a flint and steel, as our own fathers and mothers did one hundred years ago, and before they had flint and steel they used rubbing-sticks." We have all read about bringing fire out of two sticks by rubbing them together. I tried it once for an hour, and I know now I never would have got it in a thousand years as I was doing it. Others have had the same experience; consequently, most persons look upon this as a sort of fairy tale, or, if they believe it to be true, they think it so difficult as to be worth no second thought. All wood-crafters, I find, are surprised and greatly interested to learn that not only is it possible, it is easy to make a friction fire, if you know how, and hopeless, if you don't. I have taught many boys and men (including some Indians) to do it, and some have grown so expert that they make it nearly as quickly as with an old-fashioned sulphur match. When I first learned from Walter Hough, who learned from the Indians, it took me from five to ten minutes to get a blazing fire—not half an hour, as some books have it. But later I got it down to a minute, then to thirty-one seconds, from the time of taking up the rubbing sticks to having a fine blaze; the time in getting the first spark being about six seconds.

My early efforts were inspired by book accounts of Indian methods, but, unfortunately, I have never yet seen a book account that was accurate enough to guide any one successfully in the art of fire-making. All omit one or other of the absolute essentials, or dwell on some triviality. The impression they leave on those who know is that the writers did not.

The surest and easiest method of making a friction fire is by

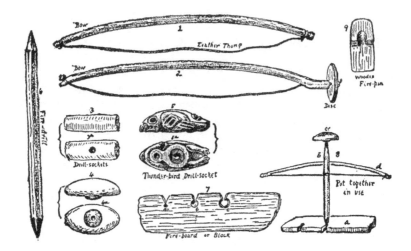

THE RUBBING-STICKS FOR FIRE-MAKING

1. The simplest kind of bow; a bent stick with a stout leather thong fastened at each end. It is about 27 inches long and ⅝ inch thick.

2. A more elaborate bow with a hole at each end for the thong. At the handle end it goes through a disc of wood. This is to tighten the thong by pressure of the hand against the disc while using.

3. Simplest kind of drill-socket; a pine or hemlock knot with a shallow hole or pit in it. 3a is under view of same. It is about 4½ inches long.

4. A more elaborate drill-socket; a pebble cemented with gum in a wooden holder. 4a is under view of same.

5. A very elaborate drill-socket; it is made of tulip wood, carved to represent the Thunderbird. It has eyes of green felspar cemented in with resin. On the under side (5a) is seen, in the middle, a soapstone socket let into the wood and fastened with pine gum, and on the head a hole kept filled with grease, to grease the top of the drill before use.

6. The drill; 12 to 18 inches long and about ¾ inch thick; it is roughly eight-sided so the thong will not slip, and pointed at each end. The best wood for the drill is old, dry brash, but not punky balsam fir or cottonwood roots; but basswood, white cedar, red cedar, tamarack, and sometimes even white pine, will do.

7. Fire-board or block; about ¾ inch thick and any length handy; a is notch with pit just begun, b shows the pit after once using and in good trim for a second time, c shows the pit bored through and now useless; the notch is ½ inch wide and ¾ inch deep.

8. Shows the way of using the sticks. The block (a) is held down with one foot, the end of the drill (b) is put in the pit, the drill-socket (c) is held on top in left hand, one end of the bow (d) is held in the right hand, while the bow is drawn back and forth.

9. Is a little wooden fire-pan, not essential but convenient; its thin edge is put under the notch to catch the powder that falls.

use of the bow-drill. Two sticks, two tools, and some tinder are needed.

The two sticks are the drill and the fire-board, or fire-block. The books generally tell us that these must be of different kinds of wood. This is a mistake. I have uniformly gotten the best results with two pieces of the same kind,—all the better, indeed, if they are parts of the same stick.

What kind of wood.—This is a very important question, as woods that are too hard, too soft, too wet, too oily, too gummy or too resinous, will not produce fire. The wood should be soft enough to wear away, else it produces no punk, and hard enough to wear slowly, or the heat is not enough to light the punk, and, of course, it should be highly inflammable. Those that I have had the best luck with are balsam-fir, cottonwood roots, tamarack, European larch, red cedar, white cedar, Oregon cedar, basswood, cypress, and sometimes second-growth white pine. It should always be a dry, sound stick, brash, but not in the least punky.

In each part of the country there seems to be a kind of wood well suited for fire-making. The Eastern Indians used cedar; the Northern Indians, cedar or balsam-fir; the plains Indians used cottonwood or sage-brush roots.

Perhaps the most reliable of all is dry and seasoned balsam-fir; either the species in the North woods, or in the Rockies, will do. It gives a fine big spark or coal in about seven seconds.

When in the grinding the dust that runs out of the notch is coarse and brown, it means that the wood is too soft; when it is very fine and scanty it means that the wood is too hard.

I have made many experiments to determine whether there is anything in the idea that it is better to have the block and the drill of different woods.

But no hybrid combination was so successful as " two of a kind."

The drill and the bow and socket are fully described in the plate.

The preparing of the fire-board is one of the most important things. At the edge cut a notch half an inch wide and about three-fourths of an inch deep; at the top of this notch make a pit or shallow hole, and the board is ready. The importance of this notch is such that it is useless to try fire-making without it.

While these are the essentials, it is well to get ready, also, some *tinder*. I have tried a great many different kinds of lint and punk, including a number that were artificially prepared, soaked with saltpetre or other combustibles. But these are not really fair play. The true woodcrafter limits himself to the things that he can get in the woods, and in all my recent fire-making I have contented myself with the tinder used for ages by the Redmen: that is, cedarwood finely shredded between two stones. Some use the fringes that grow on birch, improving it by rubbing in powdered charcoal.

Now that he has the tools and material ready, it will be an easy matter for the matchless castaway to produce a fire.

Pass the leather thong once around the drill—and this should make the thong taut; put the lower point of the drill in the pit at the top of the notch in the fire-board, and hold the socket with the left hand, on top of the drill. The notch of the fire-board should be resting on a chip or thin wooden tray. Hold the bow by the handle end in the right hand, steady the board under the left foot, and the left arm against the left knee (see Fig. 5). Now draw the bow back and forth with steady, even strokes, its full length. This causes the drill to turn in the pit and bore into the wood; ground-up wood runs out of the side of the notch, falling on the chip or tray. At first it is brown; in two or three seconds it turns black, and then smokes; in five or six seconds it is giving off a cloud of smoke. A few more vigorous strokes of the bow, and now it will be found that smoke still comes from the pile of black wood-dust on the chip (Fig. 6). Fan this gently with the hand; the smoke increases, and in a few seconds you see a glowing coal in the middle of the dust. (There are never any visible flying sparks.)

Now take a liberal pinch of the cedar tinder—about a teaspoonful; wrap this in some bark-fibre or shredded rope to keep it from blowing away. Hold it down on the coal, and lifting tray and all, blow or fan it until in a few seconds it blazes. Carefully pile over it the shreds of birch-bark or splinters of fat pine prepared beforehand, and the fire is made.

If you have the right wood and still cannot get the fire, it is likely because you do not hold the drill steady, or have not cut the side notch quite into the middle point of the little fire-pit.

The advantages of learning this method are threefold:

First—Fire-making by friction is an interesting experiment in woodcraft.

Second—A boy is better equipped having learned it. He can never afterward freeze to death for lack of matches if he has wood and an old shoe-lace.

Third—For the very reason that it is difficult, compared with matches, it tends to prevent the boys making unnecessary fires, and thus reduces the danger of their setting the woods ablaze or of smoking the forbidden cigarette.

There is such a fascination in making the rubbing-stick fire that one of my Western cooks, becoming an expert, gave up the use of matches for a time and lit his morning fire with the fire-drill, and, indeed, he did not find it much slower than the usual way.

Walter Hough told me a story of an Apache Indian who scoffed at the matches of white men, and claimed that he could light a fire with rubbing-sticks faster than Hough could with matches. So each made ready. They were waiting for the word "go" when the Indian said:

"Wait. I see if him right." He gave a few strokes with the drill, and called—"Stop—stop—him no good." He re-arranged the sticks, and tried a few more strokes. Just as Mr. Hough was going to strike the match, he said: "Stop—stop—him no good." He did this three times before he called "Ready." Then the word "go" was given. The white man struck the slow, sizzling match. The Indian gave half a dozen twirls to the drill—the smoke burst forth. He covered it with the tinder, fanned a few seconds, then a bright flame arose, just before the white man got his twigs ablaze. So the Indian won, but it was by an Indian trick; for the three times when he pretended to be trying it, he was really warming up the wood—that is, doing a large part of the work. I am afraid that, deft as he was, he would have lost in a fair race. Yet this incident shows at least that, in point of speed, the old rubbing-sticks are not so very far behind the matches as one might have supposed.

It is, indeed, a wonder that the soldiers at West Point are not taught this simple trick, when it is so easily learned, and might some day be the one thing to save the lives of many of them.

WHAT TO DO WHEN LOST IN THE WOODS

(*L. H. Journal,* October, 1902)

" Did you ever get lost in the woods? " I once asked a company of twenty campers. Some answered, " Yes; once or twice ";
others said, " Many a time." Only two said, " No, never." Then
I said, turning to the two, " I know that all the others here have
had plenty of experience, and that you two are the tenderfeet,
and never lived in the woods."

It is quite certain to come soon or late; if you go camping, you
will get lost in the woods. Hunters, Indians, yes, birds and
beasts, get lost at times. You can avoid it for long by always
taking your bearings and noting the landscape before leaving
the camp, and this you should always do; but still you will get
lost some time, and it is well to be ready for it by carrying
matches, knife, and compass.

When you do miss your way, the first thing to remember is,
like the Indian, " *You* are not lost; it is the *teepee* that is lost."
It isn't serious. It cannot be unless you do something foolish.

The first and most natural thing to do is to get on a hill, up
a tree, or other high lookout, and seek for some landmark near
camp. You may be sure of this:

You are not nearly so far from camp as you think you are.

Your friends will soon find you.

You can help them best by signalling.

The worst thing you can do is to get frightened. The truly
dangerous enemy is not the cold or the hunger so much as the
fear. It is fear that robs the wanderer of his judgment and of
his limb power; it is fear that turns the passing experience into
a final tragedy. Only keep cool and all will be well.

If there is snow on the ground, you can follow your back track.

If you see no landmark, look for the smoke of the fire. Shout
from time to time, and wait; for though you have been away
for hours it is quite possible you are within earshot of your

friends. If you happen to have a gun, fire it off twice in quick succession on your high lookout; then wait and listen. Do this several times and wait plenty long enough—perhaps an hour. If this brings no help, send up a distress signal—that is, make two smoke fires by smothering two bright fires with green leaves and rotten wood, and keep them at least fifty feet apart, or the wind will confuse them. Two shots or two smokes are usually understood to mean " I am in trouble." Those in camp on seeing this should send up one smoke, which means " Camp is here."

If you have a dog or a horse with you, you may depend upon it he can bring you out all right; but usually you will have to rely on yourself. The simplest plan, when there is fresh snow and no wind, is to follow your own track back. No matter how far around or how crooked it may be, it will certainly bring you out safely.

If you are sure of the general direction to the camp and determined to keep moving, leave a note pinned on a tree if you have paper; if not, write with charcoal on a piece of wood, and also make a good smoke, so that you can come back to this spot if you choose. But make certain that the fire cannot run, by clearing the ground around it and by banking it around with sods. And mark your course by breaking or cutting a twig every fifty feet. You can keep straight by the sun, the moon, or the stars, but when they are unseen you must be guided by the compass. I do not believe much in guidance by what are called Nature's compass signs. It is usual to say, for example, that the north side of the tree has the most moss, or the south side the most limbs, etc. While these are true in general, there are so many exceptions that when alarmed, and in doubt as to which is north, one is not in a frame of mind to decide with certainty on such fine points.

If a strong west wind, for example, was blowing when you left camp, and has blown ever since, you can be pretty sure it is still a west wind; but the only safe and certain natural compass guides are the sun, moon, and stars.

The Pole or North Star, and the Great Bear (also called the Dipper and the Pointers), should be known to every boy as they are to every Indian. The Pointers always point out the

Pole-star. Of course, they go around it once in twenty-four hours, so this makes a kind of clock.

The stars, then, will enable you to keep straight if you travel. But thick woods, fog, or clouds are apt to come up, and without something to guide you are sure to go around in a circle.

Old woodsmen commonly follow down the streams. These are certain to bring you out somewhere; but the very worst travelling is along the edges of the streams, and they take you a long way around. All things considered, it is usually best to stay right where you are, especially if in a wild country where there is no chance of finding a farmhouse. Make yourself confortable for the night by gathering plenty of good wood while it is daylight, and building a wind screen on three sides, with the fire in front, and something to keep you off the ground. Do not worry, but keep up a good fire; and when day comes renew your two smokes and wait. A good fire is the best friend of a lost man.

I have been lost a number of times, but always got out without serious trouble, because I kept cool. The worst losing I ever got was after I had been so long in the West that I qualified to act as a professional guide, and was engaged by a lot of Eastern farmers looking for land locations.

This was in the October of 1883 on the Upper Assiniboin. The main body of the farmers had remained behind. I had gone ahead with two of them. I took them over hundreds of miles of wild country. As we went northward the country improved. We were travelling with oxen, and it was our custom to let them graze for two hours at noon. One warm day, while the oxen were feeding, we went in our shirt-sleeves to a distant butte that promised a lookout. We forgot about the lateness till the sun got low. Even then I could have got back to camp, but clouds came up and darkness fell quickly. Knowing the general direction I kept on, and after half an hour's tramp we came to a cañon I had never seen before. I got out my compass and a match and found that I had been circling, as one is sure to do in the dark. I corrected the course and led off again. After another brief turn I struck another match and learned from the compass that I was again circling. This was discouraging, but with corrected course we again tramped. I was leading, and suddenly the dark ground ten feet ahead of me turned gray. I could not make it out, so went cautiously nearer. I lay down, reached forth, and then slowly made sure that we were on the edge of a steep precipice. I backed off, and frankly told the men I did not know where we were. I got out my match-box and compass and found I had but one match left.

"Any of you got any matches?" I asked. "No; left 'em all in our coats," was their answer.

"Well," said I, "I have one. Shall I use it to get a new course from the compass, or shall we make a fire and stay here till morning?"

All voted to camp for the night. There was now a cold rain. We groped into a hollow where we got some dead wood, and by using our knives got some dry chips from the inside of a log. When all was ready we gathered close around, and I got out the one match. I was about to strike it when the younger of the men said:

"Say, Seton, you are not a smoker; Jack is. Hadn't you better give him that match?"

There was sense in this. I have never in my life smoked. Jack was an old stager and an adept with matches. I handed it to him. "*Rrrp—fizz*"—and in a minute we had a fire.

With the help of the firelight we now found plenty of dead wood; we made three blazing fires side by side, and after an hour we removed the centre one, then raked away all the hot ashes, and all lay down together on the warm ground. When the morning came the rain ceased. We stretched our stiffened limbs and made for camp. Yes, there it was in plain view two miles away across a fearful cañon. Three steps more on that gloomy night and we should have been over the edge of that cañon and dashed to the botton.

FIRST AID TO THE INJURED

American National Red Cross textbook, 30 cents

To prepare in First Aid to the Injured, scouts should follow a definite course of study and practice under a qualified leader, preferably a physician. Much care should be observed to prevent scouts from doing things in case of accident or emergency which might be dangerous to the sufferer. It should be remembered that an elementary course does not prepare for expert service. To make this work as thorough as possible, leaders and scouts will wisely follow the course prescribed by the American National Red Cross, and the International Committee of the Young Men's Christian Association. Upon completing the course the scout may pass the regular examination and secure the joint certificate of these organizations.

The regular button, badge, or insignia of the Boy Scouts will be awarded only upon the successful completion of this work, and of the examination. Leaders should familiarize themselves with that which follows. Additional information may be secured from the Educational Department of the International Committee of Y. M. C. A., 124 East Twenty-eighth Street, New York.

The Course. Each instructor is encouraged to use any course with which he can best cover the topics below. The following is suggested for ten sessions:

1. Structure and important functions of the human body; skeleton, muscles, circulation system, respiration system. General directions for First Aid.

2. Simple First Aid materials—bandages, splints, stimulants, emetics.

3. Common accidents—as bruises, sprains, dislocations, broken bones, fractures; wounds, severed arteries, hemorrhage, rabies. Prevention of accidents. Practice work.

4. Injuries by foreign bodies in eye, throat, nose, and ear; burns and scalds, fainting, fits, lockjaw, poisoning. Prevention. Practice work.

5. Sunstroke and heat exhaustion, frost-bite and freezing; in-

jury from electricity and lightning. Prevention. Practice work.

6. Common emergencies—as drowning, cramp, diarrhea, constipation, vomiting, hiccough, nervous attack. Practice work. Emergency supplies.

7. Croup, neuralgia in face, toothache, earache, styes, chilblains. Emergency supplies. Practice work.

8. Vocational accidents. Special attention given the more common injuries of men forming the majority of the class— as accidents peculiar to men in shop and factory, to those in railroad service, in the mine, on the farm, in business, etc. Prevention of accidents. Practice work.

9. Injuries of indoor and outdoor sports—gymnasium, baseball, football, boating, swimming, shooting, fishing, etc. Prevention. Much practice.

10. Transportation of the wounded, injured, and sick. Much practice.

Suggestions. In the majority of cases the best work is found when:

1. The leader or instructor is an active, successful physician, the physical director, or some other similarly trained person.

2. Ten or fifteen sessions of the group or class have been held —one per week for ten or fifteen weeks, or two per week for six or eight weeks, or if in camp or summer school, one session per day for ten or fifteen days.

3. The course involves talks, demonstrations, and quizzes by the leader, and much of both written and practice work by students. Each session should involve some practice in bandaging; reducing fractures, dislocations; dressing burns, wounds; severed arteries; treatment for drowning, epilepsy, etc.

4. Any textbook may be used. The new textbook prepared by the American National Red Cross, with particular reference to the above course, is recommended. Price 30c. While desirable for each student to have a text, yet one book is often used among several students.

5. The American National Red Cross attaches much emphasis —(a) to practice or demonstration work of the student in both the course of study and the examination, (b) to preventive meas-

ures against accident. Attention given to prevention is one of the best investments.

6. Emergency boxes or outfits may be secured of dealers in medical, surgical or first aid supplies, or scouts may easily provide themselves with triangular and strip bandages, safety pins, plaster, etc. The International Committee and the Red Cross are arranging for small outfits or kits for group or individual use. Particulars may be secured upon application, 124 East Twenty-eighth Street, New York.

The Examination. It includes questions or tests in both written and practice work. Both must be given at the one session, the written usually preceding the practice work. The student selects and answers in writing any six of the ten questions, using paper, letter size 8 x 11 in. (furnished by the International Committee). This part of the examination, when perfect, is worth 60 credits. For the practice work the local instructor specifies four tests from the question paper so that as far as possible no two students will have the same exercises. This practice work part of the examination, when perfect, is worth 40 credits.

At the top of the sheet should appear date, student's name, and the teacher's grade mark for the examination—both the written and practice work. The examination for both members and non-members of the Y. M. C. A. will be held by the association in case there is one in community.

Dates. The official examinations are held on some specific evening in April, June,—July and August for campers,—and December. The exact days are named several weeks in advance. Special examinations at other dates may be arranged in advance and, of course, at much higher rates. No results accepted if held at other dates than those specified or previously arranged. The time required is usually less than two hours—forty-five minutes for the written and sixty minutes for the practice work—and between 6 and 11 P. M. Exact dates for the examinations may be secured from the local Y. M. C. A. See paragraph (h) below.

Cost. Thirty-five cents (25c. to association members) for each question paper ordered. No order accepted for less than four papers. The cost of conducting the examination is much greater than the receipts from such fees. This charge includes the questions, the blank paper for each person, printed forms, and the certificate, if won.

How to Order Questions. Only one person is permitted to use a single question paper. The mistake often made is in not ordering enough papers. The examiner will accept no more answer papers than there were question papers ordered. Orders must reach George B. Hodge, 124 East Twenty-eighth Street, ten days prior to date of examination. *Be specific as to whom the papers are to be sent, and where.* Orders must be official. Patrols desiring to participate in the examination should send for Requisition Blanks early enough, so that the official order may reach the above address ten days preceding the date of the examination desired.

Some Suggestions. (*a*) Send in order early, and for no less than four papers. Send cash with the order.

(*b*) Envelopes containing question papers must not be opened until the specified hour for the examination, and then only in the presence of the class.

(*c*) Every one concerned in the conduct of the examination should become familiar with all details concerning it in order to avoid error and delay.

(*d*) The Class List containing the names of students marked 65 or above, must be signed by the secretary or director to the effect that all regulations, covering the examination, have been faithfully observed, before such results can be accepted by the examiner.

(*e*) Violation of any regulation cancels the examination and no resulting papers from such examination can be accepted.

(*f*) If the class is large, one or more deputies, as physicians or the leaders' corps, may aid the local examiner in the practice tests.

(*g*) The examination in the summer time may be held at the camp or in the summer school in the daytime, or at the local association in the evening, but it must be held on the date specified.

(*h*) Additional information and directions, together with former question papers, will be sent upon application. With the official examination package will be sent the printed directions concerning the marking of papers, conduct of examinations, etc. These should be read and carefully observed.

The American
National Red Cross

First Aid Certificate

The International
Committee of

Young Men's
Christian Associations

This Certifies that ___John Benton___

has satisfactorily completed the elementary course of study and
passed the official examinations in **FIRST AID TO THE INJURED**

For the American Red Cross:

Wm H Taft
PRESIDENT.

Chas. L. Magee
Secretary.

WASHINGTON, D. C.

For the International Committee,
Educational Department:

Frederic B Pratt
CHAIRMAN

Geo D Pratt
Secretary

NEW YORK, N. Y.

___April___ 1910

LIFE-SAVING IN WATER

By Geo. J. Fisher

1. Every boy who learns to swim 100 yards is to receive an award.

2. Every boy who teaches another boy to swim 100 yards, to receive an award.

3. I would suggest the following as a test for life-saving award. This is usually the kind of a test provided by the U. S. Volunteer Life-Saving Corps.

Swimming Ability:

Carry person of own weight 3 ways in 10 yards.
Swim with suit of clothes on.
Swim 100 yards on back, no hands.
200 yards straightway—breast and side.
Dive and fetch in 10 feet of water or 7 feet.

Care of Apparatus:

How do you hand up a buoy?   (Show with buoy.)

After an accident case, what is done with the contents of the chest?

If an oar or boat-part is missing, what is done?

Who should be permitted to use the boat?

How should you leave a lifeboat when the tide is dropping?

Boat Work:

What is a thwart?   Rowlock?   Thole pine?   Painter? Amidships?

Define starboard; port; aft.

Who is the first out of a boat, and the last man in?

Make clove hitch or two half-hitches.   Tie a square knot.

Explain boat-orders: Give way together; hold water; trail; stern all; up oars; let fall.

The Life-Saving Corps offers a button for an auxiliary membership to every person who passes a test similar to this.

THE STARS

As Seen with the Naked Eye

(The chief works referred to in this are C. Flammarion's " Popular Astronomy " (Gore's translation), and Garrett P. Serviss' "Astronomy with an Opera Glass." Those who wish to go further a-sky are referred to these books.)

Whether he expects to use them as guides or not, every boy should learn the principal constellations and the important stars. A non-scientific friend said to me once: " I am always glad that I learned the principal star groups when I was young. I have never forgotten them, and, no matter in what strange country I find myself, I can always look up at night, and see the old familiar stars that shone on me in my home in my own country."

All American boys know the Dipper or Great Bear. This is, perhaps, the most important star group in our sky, because of its size, peculiar form, and the fact that it never sets in our latitude, and last, that it always points out the Pole-star, and, for this reason, it is sometimes known as the Pointers. It is called the Dipper because it is shaped like a dipper with a long, bent handle. Why it is called the Great Bear is not so easy to explain. The classical legend has it that the nymph Calisto, having violated her vow, was changed by Diana into a bear, which, after death, was immortalized in the sky by Zeus. Another suggestion is that the earliest astronomers, the Chaldeans, called these stars " the shining ones," and their word happened to be very like the Greek *arktos* (a bear). Another explanation (I do not know who is authority for either) is that vessels in olden days were named for animals, etc. They bore at the prow the carved effigy of the namesake, and, if the Great Bear, for example, made several very happy voyages by setting out when a certain constellation was in the ascendant, that constellation might become known as the Great Bear's constellation. Certainly, there is nothing in its shape to justify the name. Very few of the constellations, indeed, are like the thing they are called after. Their names were usually given for some fanciful association with the namesake, rather than for resemblance to it.

The Pole-star is really the most important of the stars in our sky: it marks the north at all times; it alone is fixed in the heavens; all the other stars seem to swing around it once in twenty-four hours. It is in the end of the Little Bear's tail. But the Pole-star, or Polaris, is not a very bright one, and it would be hard to identify but for the help of the Dipper, or Pointers.

The outer side (Alpha and Beta) of the Dipper points nearly to Polaris, at a distance equal to three and one-half times the space that separates these two stars of the Dipper's outer side.

Various Indians call the Pole-star the " Home Star " and " The Star that Never Moves," and the Dipper they call the " Broken Back."

The last star but one in the Dipper, away from the pole—that is, the star at the bend of the handle,—is known to astronomers as Mizar, one of the Horses. Just above it, and tucked close in, is a smaller star known to astronomers as Alcor, or the Rider. The Indians call these two the " Old Squaw and the Pappoose on Her Back." In the old world, from very ancient times, these have been used as tests of eyesight. To be able to see Alcor with the naked eye means that one has excellent eyesight. So also on the plains, the old folks would ask the children at night, " Can you see the pappoose on the old squaw's back? " and when the youngster saw it, and proved that he did by a right description, they rejoiced that he had the eyesight which is the first requisite of a good hunter.

The Great Bear is also to be remembered as the Pointers for another reason. It is the hour-hand of the woodman's clock. It goes once around the North Star in about twenty-four hours, same way as the sun, and for the same reason—that it is the earth that is going and leaving them behind.

The time in going around is not exactly twenty-four hours, so that the position of the Pointer varies with the seasons, but, as a rule, this for woodcraft purposes is near enough. The bowl

of the Dipper swings one and one-half times the width of the
opening (*i.e.,* fifteen degrees) in one hour. If it went a quarter
of the circle, that would mean you had slept a quarter of a day,
or six hours.

Each fifteen days the stars seem to be an hour earlier, in three
months they gain one-fourth of the circle, and in a year gain
the whole circle.

According to Flammarion, there are about 7,000 stars visible
to the naked eye, and of those but nineteen are stars of the first
magnitude.   Thirteen of them are visible in the latitude of New
York, the other six belong to the South Polar Region of the
sky.   Here is Flammarion's arrangement of them in order of
seeming brightness.   Those that can be seen in the Southern
Hemisphere only, are in brackets:

1. Sirius, the Dog-star.
2. (Canopus, of Argo.)
3. (Alpha, of the Centaur.)
4. Arcturus, of Boötes.
5. Vega, of the Lyre.
6. Rigel, of Orion's foot.
7. Capella, of Auriga.
8. Procyon, or the Little Dog-star.
9. Betelgeuse, of Orion's right shoulder.
10. (Beta, of the Centaur.)
11. (Achernar, of Eridanus.)
12. Aldebaran, of Taurus, the Bull's right eye.
13. Antares, of Scorpio.
14. (Alpha, of the Southern Cross.)
15. Altair, of the Eagle.
16. Spica, of Virgo.
17. Fomalhaut, of the Southern Fish.
18. (Beta, of the Southern Cross.)
19. Regulus, of the Lion.

1. SIRIUS (Sir'-i-us), of *Canis Major,* the Dog-star, the
Nile Star. It is a delicate green and by far the brightest star
in the sky. It is placed in the head of Orion's hound, whence
its name. It is nearly on a line with Orion's belt, away from
the pole, and as far from the end of the belt as Betelgeuse is

from Rigel, that is, about two Dipper-rims; it is three total Dipper-lengths from the Dipper on a line drawn from the inner rim through the middle of the outer side.

It is nearly in a line with Aldebaran and Betelgeuse, and as far from the latter as it is from the former. Sirius is a wonderfully bright star, really 70 times as brilliant as the sun, is 20 times as large, and about 500,000 times as far from the earth as the sun is (*Serviss*). That is, if 1 inch stands for our distance from the sun, then Sirius is 7 miles from us. Long supposed to be the nearest and the greatest of all the fixed stars, but Canopus in the Southern Hemisphere is known to be vastly greater, probably the greatest of all. Alpha of the Centaur is much nearer. The Dog-star has a dark companion.

2. (CANOPUS (Ca-no'-pus), of Argo.) Supposed to be the greatest of the stars, probably 300 or 400 times as large as our Sun; not visible in the North.

3. (ALPHA, of the Centaur.) The nearest of the stars. Not visible in the Northern States (*Flammarion*, p. 304).

4. ARCTURUS (Arc-tu'-rus). A red or orange star in Boötes. Continue the curve of the handle of the Dipper, about the total length of the Dipper, and it leads to Arcturus. Boötes is the Bear-hunter, because it chases the Polar Bear around the Pole. Arcturus, Denebola, and Spica make an equilateral triangle. It is one of the few near enough to the Earth to have its distance measured. The three great stars in the north are Arcturus, Vega, and Capella.

5. VEGA (Ve'-ga). A bluish-white star in Lyra. Draw a line from the inner bottom corner of the body of the Dipper through the first star to the handle from the Dipper— continue it twice the total length of the Dipper and you come to Vega.

"In 12,000 years Vega will be close to the pole, as it was 14,000 years ago" (*F.*). Serviss says Vega is the most magnificent of all the stars to which the rôle of Pole-star can fall.

6. RIGEL (Ri'-gel). A bluish-white star in Orion. Draw a line across the brim of the Dipper, away from the handle and as long as three times the length of the whole Dipper, and it ends at Rigel, in the left foot of the Giant Hunter Orion. " Rigel

is one of the most beautiful double stars in the sky, having a little blue companion close under its wing " (*S.*).

Too far to be measured; shows scarcely any motion. The same remarks apply to Canopus, Betelgeuse, Achernar, Antares, Spica, and Alpha Cygni.

7. CAPELLA (Ca-pel'-la), of Auriga. A line drawn across the brim of the Dipper, beginning at the handle side and carried on one and one-half times the length of the Dipper to the other side of the Pole-star ends nearly at Capella. A line from Pollux, through Castor, also points nearly to Capella. Capella means the she-goat; with its three kids (small stars) it forms an isosceles triangle.

8. PROCYON (Pro-cy'-on), of *Canis Minor*, the Little Dog-star. A line drawn from the inner rim of the Dipper, through the outer lower corner, and on for twice the Dipper's total length, touches Procyon, the Little Dog-star.

A line drawn from Bellatrix through Betelgeuse, and on twice as far as they are apart, reaches Procyon. Procyon, Castor, and the Pole-star are nearly on a line, of which two-thirds is between Castor and the pole. It is a white star and is going from us (*F.*). Both the Dog-stars are dogged by a dark, invisible companion.

9. BETELGEUSE (Bet-el-gerz'), of Orion, is an orange star. Draw a line through the two bottom stars of the Dipper, away from the handle, rather more than twice the total length of the Dipper, and it ends at Betelgeuse, in the Giant Orion's right shoulder. " Slightly variable. Too far to measure; no perceptible motion" (*F.*). " Sometimes it seems brighter than Rigel, and sometimes less brilliant. Orange stars twinkle least; white most " (*S.*).

10. (BETA, of the Centaur.) Not visible in the North.

11. (ACHERNAR (A-ker'ner), of Eridanus.) Cannot be seen in the northern latitudes.

12. ALDEBARAN (Al-deb'-a-ran). A splendid red star in Taurus. It is the right eye of the Bull, one of the blazing lamps of winter. It is about as far from Betelgeuse as Betelgeuse is from Rigel; the three together make a right-angle, with Aldebaran nearest to the pole. It is the chief star of the Hyades that are on the head of the Bull.

13. ANTARES (An-ta'-rez). A deep-red star, the chief one in Scorpio, which is on a line drawn from the front bottom corner of the Dipper, through the end of the handle, three total Dipper-lengths, touches Antares. It can be seen by us only in summer, and is low in the southern sky. "In the last visible stage of cooling" (*Lockyer*). "Almost extinct" (*S.*).

14. (ALPHA, of the Southern Cross) cannot be seen in the northern latitudes.

15. ALTAIR (Al-tair'), of the Eagle, a diamond-white star. Draw a line from Mizar to Vega, then one-half as far again, and it touches Altair.

16. SPICA (Spi'-ka), of Virgo, a diamond-white star. A line drawn from the Pole Star through the first star in the handle of the Dipper, away from the bowl, carried on about two total Dipper-lengths farther, reaches Spica. Or, the Dipper-handle curves on to Arcturus, and carry the same curve on as far again, and it reaches Spica.

DENEBOLA (De-neb'-o-la) is in the Lion's tail; with Spica and Arcturus, it marks the corners of a great equilateral triangle, "remarkable for its pure white light; . . . no companion star in the sky equal to it in this respect" (*S.*).

It is so far away, we can neither compute its motion nor its distance.

17. FOMALHAUT (Fo'-mal-o), of the Southern Fish, a star of autumn, seen far down to the south.

When the outer edge of the Dipper is straight under the pole, Fomalhaut is due south.

The line of the Pointers through the Pole-star, continued across the heavens about three and one-half total Dipper-lengths beyond, touches Fomalhaut. It is a lonely star, no other bright one being near. Is one of the stars important to the mariner (*S.*).

18. (BETA, of the Southern Cross) cannot be seen in northern latitudes.

19. REGULUS, of the Lion, a white star. Follow the front and back sides of the Dipper downwards and backwards till they meet, that is, about one and one-half total Dipper-lengths, and they reach Regulus. This star is also in the end of the handle

of a great sickle whose main line, leaving off the small half of the hook, points to the Pole-star.

SOME REMARKABLE STARS OF THE SECOND MAGNITUDE

The Pole-star, considered by some as the most important of all, is graded by its light as a star of the second magnitude only. All the other stars turn around it once in twenty-four hours.

The outer rim of the Dipper points nearly to it, at about a

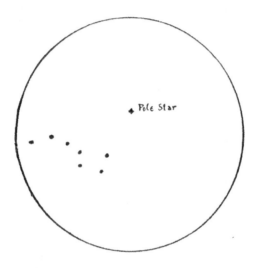

whole Dipper-length distance. There is no other bright star near it, so it is easy to find.

The Pole-star is not so fixed as it seems. When the great Pyramid was built, 4,000 years ago, Alpha Draconis was the Pole-star. The long north tube in the Pyramid exactly pointed to this star at its lowest point (*F.*, p. 39). Alpha Draconis is a third magnitude star, in line with the inner wall of the Dipper, at twice the length of the Dipper's side from the rim.

ALGOL (Al'-gol), the Demon Star, B. Perseus. Draw a line

from the bottom back star of the Dipper (Gamma) through the outer rim star of the same (Alpha), about two and one-half Dipper-lengths, and it ends at Algol, or a line from the last star of the Dipper-handle through the Pole-star, and as far on the other side, ends also at Algol. This is a wonderful, variable star that changes from about second to about fourth magnitude in less than three days. For two and one-half days it is constant, then it begins to fade, and in two and one-half hours is down to fourth magnitude; remains so for about fifteen minutes; then in three and one-half hours is restored to second magnitude. This change is supposed to be caused by a dark planet passing over it.

It was formerly red; now white (*Gore*).

MIZAR (My'-zar). Zeta of Ursa Major. This is the middle star of the Dipper-handle, the one that marks the curve. Close above Mizar is a very small star which can be seen by very keen eyes unaided by glasses. This little star is Alcor.

These two are called the Horse and Rider, or, among the Indians, the Squaw and Pappoose.

THE CONSTELLATIONS

ORION (O-ri'on), with its striking array of brilliant stars, Betelgeuse, Rigel, the Three Kings, etc., is generally admitted to be the finest constellation in the heavens.

Orion was the hunter giant who went to Heaven when he died, and now marches around the great dome, but is seen only

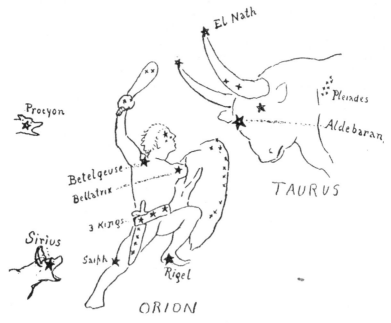

in the winter, because, during the summer, he passes over during daytime. Thus he is still the hunter's constellation. The three stars of his belt are called the "Three Kings."

Sirius, the Great Dog-star, is in the head of Orion's hound, and following farther back is the Little Dog-star, Procyon.

In old charts of the stars, Orion is shown with his hound, hunting the bull, Taurus.

PLEIADES (Ply'-a-des). Can be seen in winter as a cluster of small stars between Aldebaran and Algol, or, a line drawn from the back-bottom, through the front-rim of the Dipper, about two Dipper-lengths, touches this little group. They are not far from Aldebaran, being on the shoulder of the Bull, of which Aldebaran is the right eye. They may be considered the seven arrow wounds made by Orion. They are nearer the Pole-star than Aldebaran is, and on the side away from the Dipper; also, they are nearly on a line between Beta of the Dipper (front bottom) and Capella.

Serviss tells us that the Pleiades have a supposed connection with the Great Pyramid, because " about 2170 B. C., when the beginning of spring coincided with the culmination of the Pleiades at midnight, that wonderful group of stars was visible just at midnight, through the mysterious southward-pointing passage of the Pyramid."

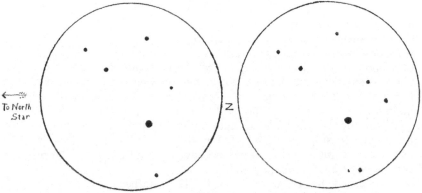

To North Star

The Pleiades as seen with the best of naked eyes

PLEIADES AS A TEST OF EYESIGHT

This star-group has always been considered a good test of eyesight.

I once asked a group of boys in camp how many of the Pleiades they could count with the naked eye. A noisy, forward boy, who was nicknamed " Bluejay," because he was so fond of chatting and showing off, said, " Oh, I see hundreds."

" Well, you can sit down," I said, " for you can do nothing of the kind."

Another steadier boy said, " I believe I see six," and he proved that he did see them, for he mapped them out properly on a board with six pebbles.

That boy had good eyes, because poor eyes see merely a haze, but another boy present had better eyes, for he saw, and proved that he saw, seven. This is considered first-class. The Indians as a rule see seven, because they call them the Seven Stars. But, according to Flammarion, it is possible to exceed this, for several persons have given proof that they distinguished ten Pleiades. This is almost the extreme of human eyesight. There is, however, according to the same authority, a record of thirteen Pleiades having been actually seen by the unaided human eye.

The telescope reveals some 2,000 in the cluster.

The Indians call them the " Seven Dancers," and tell a legend that seems to explain their dancing about the smallest one, as well as the origin of the constellation.

Once there were seven little Indian boys, who used to take their bowl of succotash each night and eat their suppers together on a mound outside the village. Six were about the same size, one was smaller than the rest, but he had a sweet voice, and knew many songs, so after supper the others would dance around the mound to his singing, and he marked time on his drum.

When the frosty days of autumn were ending, and winter threatened to stop the nightly party, they said, " Let us ask our parents for some venison, so we can have a grand feast and dance for the last time on the mound."

They asked, but all were refused. Each father said, " When I was a little boy, I thought myself lucky to get even a pot of succotash, and never thought of asking for venison as well."

So the boys assembled at the mound. All were gloomy but the little singer, who said :—

" Never mind, brothers! We shall feast without venison and we shall be merry just the same, for I shall sing you a new song that shall lighten your hearts."

First, he made each of them fasten on his head a little torch

of birch-bark, then he sat down in the middle and thumped away
at his little drum and sang:

> I sing you a song, a new song,
> Of the dancing feet and heart, Ki, yi, yi;
> Dance lightly with your feet, brothers,
> For so your hearts dance too,
> Lighter and lighter,
> Ki yi, ki yi, ki yi, yi, yi, yi.
> As the young fawn danced
> Last leaf moon, Ki, yi, yi;
> Lighter and lighter;
> As the mayfly danced in the grass moon,
> Lighter and lighter,
> As the longbill skips on the haymarsh.
> Ki yi, ki yi, ki yi, yi, yi, yi.
> Lighter and lighter,
> Round and round—
> As the fireflies go in the tree tops.
> Ki yi yi.
>
> Lighter and lighter,
> Round and round—up and round,
> As the red leaves dance in the whirlwind.
> Ki yi, ki yi, ki yi, yi, yi, yi.
>
> Lighter and lighter,
> Fawns—flies—snipe—
> Faster and faster, fireflies—leaves—
> Dance, brothers, dance and leap—
> And leap and laugh; and laugh and leap
> Away to the sky, away—away and away—
> Ki yi, ki yi, ki yi, yi, yi, yi,
> Ya—hooooo—ooop——

They were fairly whirling now, and, as the singer gave this
last whoop of the last dance on the mound, they and he went
dancing over the tree tops into the sky; light of heart and heels
and head, they went, and their parents rushed out in time to see

them go, but too late to stop them. And now you may see them every clear autumn night as winter draws near; you may see the little torches sparkling as they dance, the six around the little one in the middle. Of course, you can't hear his song, or even his drum, but you must remember he is a long way off now.

There is another story of a little Indian girl called Two-Bright-Eyes. She was the only child of her parents. She wandered away one evening seeking the Whippoorwill and got lost— you see, even Indians get lost sometimes. She never returned. The mourning parents never learned what became of her, but they thought they saw a new pair of twin stars rising through the trees not long after, and when the grief was so softened by time that they could sing about it, this is the song they made about their loss :—

THE TWIN STARS

Two-Bright-Eyes went wandering out
To chase the whippoorwill.
Two-Bright-Eyes got lost, and left
Our teepee, Oh, so still!

Two-Bright-Eyes was lifted up
To sparkle in the skies,
And look like stars, but we know well
That that's our lost Bright-Eyes.

She is looking for the camp,
She would come back if she could;
She is peeping thro' the trees to find
The teepee in the wood.

THE PLANETS

The stars we see are suns like our Sun, giving out light to world that go around as our world goes around our Sun; as these worlds do not give out light, and are a long way off, we cannot see them. But around our own Sun are several worlds besides ours. They are very near to us, and we can see them by the reflected light of the Sun. These are called " planets " or " wanderers," because, before their courses were understood, they seemed to wander about, all over the sky, unlike the fixed stars.

They are so close to us that their distance and sizes are easily measured. They do not twinkle.

There are eight, in all, not counting the small Planetoids; but only those as large as stars of the first magnitude concern us. They are here in order of nearness to the Sun:—

1. MERCURY is always close to the Sun, so that it is usually lost in the glow of the twilight or of the vapors of the horizon, where it shows like a globule of quicksilver. It has phases and quarters like the Moon. It is so hot there "that a Mercurian would be frozen to death in Africa or Senegal " (*Flammarion*).

2. VENUS. The brightest of all the stars is Venus; far brighter than Sirius. It is the *Morning Star,* the *Evening Star,* the Shepherds' Star, and yet not a star at all, but a planet. It has phases and quarters like the Moon. You can place it only with the help of an almanac.

3. THE EARTH.

4. MARS. The nearest of the other worlds to us. It is a fiery-red planet. It has phases like the Moon.

5. JUPITER, like a very large star of the first magnitude, famous for its five moons, and really the largest of the planets.

6. SATURN, noted for its rings, also like a very large star of the first magnitude.

7. URANUS and (8) NEPTUNE, are too small for observation without a telescope.

THE MOON. The Moon is 1-5 the diameter of the Earth, about 1-50 of the bulk, and is about a quarter-million miles away. Its course, while very irregular, is nearly the same as the apparent course of the Sun. But " in winter the full Moon is at an altitude in the sky near the limit attained by the Sun in summer, . . . and even, at certain times, five degrees higher. It is the contrary in summer, a season when the Moon remains very low " (*F.*).

The Moon goes around the Earth in 27¼ days. It loses nearly ¾ of an hour each night; that is, it rises that much later.

FINDING YOUR LATITUDE BY THE STARS

The use of the stars to the Scout is chiefly to guide him by showing the north, but the white man has carried the use a step farther: he makes the Pole-star tell him not only where the north is, but where he himself is. From the Pole-star, he can learn his latitude.

In the Honor List it is reckoned an exploit to take one's latitude from the North Star with a cart-wheel, or with two sticks and a bucket of water. If the calculation is made within two degrees of error, it counts a simple honor; if within one degree, it counts a high honor.

The first attempt I made was with two sticks and a bucket of water. I arranged the bucket in the daytime, so that it could be filled from rim to rim, that is, it was level, and that gave me the horizon line; next, I fastened my two sticks together at an adjustable angle. Then, laying one stick across the bucket as a base, I raised the other till the two right notches on its upper edge were in straight line for the Pole-star. The sticks were now fastened at this angle and put away till the morning. On a smooth board now—the board is allowable because it can be found either far on the plains when you have your wagon, or on the ship at sea—I mapped out, first a right angle, by the old plan of measuring off a triangle, whose sides were six, eight, and ten inches, and applied the star angle to this.   By a process of equal subdivision I got 45°, 22½°, finally 40°, which seemed to be the latitude of my camp; subsequent looking-up showed it to be 41° 10'.

Of course, it is hard to imagine that the boys will ever be so placed that it is important for them to take their latitude with home-made implements; but it is also hard to imagine circumstances under which it would be necessary to know that the sun is 92,000,000 miles away.   It is very sure, however, that a boy who has once done this has a larger idea of the world and its geography, and it is likely to help him in realizing that there is some meaning to the lines and figures on the border of his school-maps, and that they are not put there merely to add to his perplexities.

SUNDIAL, OR HUNTER'S CLOCK

To make a scout's sundial, prepare a smooth board about 15 inches across, with a circle divided into 24 equal parts, and a temporarily hinged pointer, whose upper edge is in the middle of the dial.   Place on some *dead level,* solid post or stump in the open.

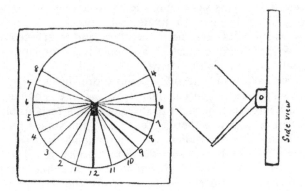

At night fix the dial so that the 12 o'clock line points exactly to north, as determined by the Pole-star.   Then, using two temporary sighting sticks of exactly the same height (so as to permit sighting clear above the edge of the board) set the pointer exactly pointing to the Pole-star, that is, the same angle as the latitude of the place, and fix it there immovably. Then, remove the two sighting sticks. As a time-piece, this dial will be found roughly correct for that latitude. The angle of the pointer, or style, must be changed for each latitude.

ARCHERY

(From *The Ladies' Home Journal*, 1902)

No woodcraft education is complete without a knowledge of Archery. It is a pity that this noble sport has fallen into disuse. We shall find it essential to some of our best games.

The modern hunting gun is an irresistible weapon of wholesale murder, and is just as deadly no matter who pulls the trigger. It spreads terror as well as death by its loud discharge, and it leaves little clew as to who is responsible for the shot. Its deadly range is so fearfully great as to put all game at the mercy of the clumsiest tyro. Woodcraft, the oldest of all sciences and one of the best, has steadily declined since the coming of the gun, and it is entirely due to this same unbridled power that America has lost so many of her fine game animals.

The bow is a far less destructive weapon, and to succeed at all in the chase the bowman must be a double-read forester. The bow is silent and it sends the arrow with exactly the same power that the bowman's arm puts into it—no more, no less—so it is really his own power that speeds the arrow. There is no question as to which hunter has the right to the game or is responsible for the shot when the arrow is there to tell. The gun stands for little skill, irresistible force supplied from an outside source, overwhelmingly unfair odds, and sure death to the victim. The bow, on the other hand, stands for all that is clever and fine in woodcraft; so, no guns or firearms of any kind are allowed in our boy Indian camp.

The Indian's bow was short, because, though less efficient, it was easier to carry than a long one. Yet it did not lack power. It is said that the arrow-head sometimes appeared on the far side of the buffalo it was fired into, and there is a tradition that Wah-

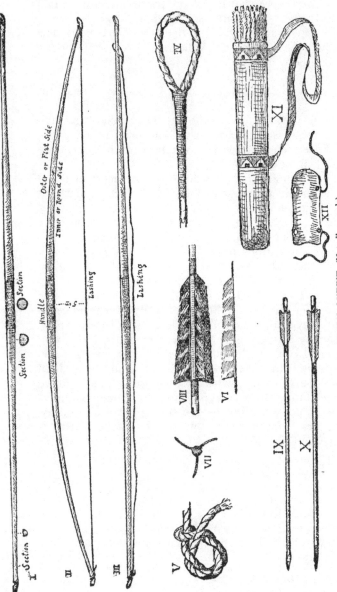

THE ARCHERY OUTFIT (Not all on scale)

I. The five-foot bow as finished, with sections at the points shown.
II. The bow "braced" or strung.
III. The bow unstrung, showing the loop slipped down.
IV. The loop that is used on the upper end of the bow.
V. The timber hitch always used on the lower end or notch of the bow.
VI. A turkey feather with split midrib, all ready to lash on.
VII. End view of arrow, showing notch and arrangement of three feathers.
VIII. Part of arrow, showing feathering and lashing.
IX. Sanger hunting arrow with wooden point; 25 inches long.
X. Sanger war arrow with nail point and extra long feathers; it also is 25 inches long.
XI. Quiver with Indian design; 20 inches long.
XII. The "bracer," or arm guard of heavy leather for left arm, with two laces to tie it on. It is six inches long.

na-tah, a Sioux chief, once shot his arrow through a cow buffalo and killed her calf that was running at the other side.

But the long bow is more effective than the short one. The old English bowmen, the best the world has ever seen, always shot with the long bow.

The finest bows and arrows are those made by the professional makers, but there is no reason why each boy should not make his own.

According to several authorities the best bow woods are mulberry, osage-orange, sassafras, Southern cedar, black locust, apple, black walnut, slippery elm, ironwood, mountain ash, hickory, California yew, and hemlock.

Take a perfectly sound, straight, well-seasoned stick 5 or 6 feet long (your bow should be about as long as yourself) ; mark off a 5-inch space in the middle for the handle; leave this round and a full inch thick; shave down the rest, flat on one side for the front and round on the other for the back, until it is about one inch wide and ¾ of an inch thick next the handle, tapering to about one-half that at the ends, which are then " nocked," nicked, or notched as shown (Cut I). These notches are for the string, which is to be put on early. Draw the bow now, flat side out, not more than the proper distance, and note carefully which end bends the most; then shave down the other side until it bends evenly. The middle scarcely bends at all. The perfect shape, when bent, is shown in Cut II. Trim the bow down to your strength and finish smoothly with sandpaper and glass. It should be straight when unstrung, and unstrung when not in use. Fancy curved bows are weak affairs. The bow for our boy should require a power of 15 or 20 pounds (shown on a spring balance) to draw the string 23 inches from the bow ; not more. The best string is of hemp or linen; it should be about 5 inches from the middle of the bow when strung (Cut II). The notches for the string should be two-thirds the depth of the string. If you have not a bought string make one of strong, unbleached linen thread twisted together. At one end the string, which is heaviest at the ends, should be fast knotted to the bow notch (Cut V) ; at the other it should have a loop as shown in Cut IV. In the middle it should be lashed with fine silk and wax for 5 inches, and the exact place marked where the arrow fits it.

The arrow is more important than the bow.   Any one can make a bow; few can make an arrow, for, as a Seminole Indian expressed it to Maurice Thompson, " Any stick do for bow; good arrow much heap work, ugh."   Hiawatha went all the way to Dakota to see the famous arrow-maker.   In England when the bow was the gun of the country, the bow-maker was called a " bowyer," and the arrow-maker a " fletcher " (from the Norman *flèche,* an arrow).   So when men began to use surnames those who excelled in arrow-making were proud to be called the " Fletchers "; but to make a good bow was not a notable achievement, hence few took " Bowyer " as their name.

The first thing about an arrow is that it must be perfectly straight.   " Straight as an arrow " refers to the arrow itself, not to its flight; that is always curved.

The Indians made arrows of reeds and of straight shoots of viburnum or arrow-wood, and of elder, but we make better arrows out of the solid heartwood of hard pine for target use, and of hickory or ash for hunting.   The arrow should be 25 inches long, round, and $\frac{3}{8}$ of an inch thick, and have 3 feathers set as shown in Cut VI, about an inch from the notch.   The feather B, that stands out at right angles to notch A, should always be away from the bow in shooting.   This is called the cock-feather, and it is usually marked or colored in some way to be quickly distinguished.

Turkey and goose wing-feathers are the best that grow in our country for arrow-feathers.   The Indians mostly use Turkey. With a sharp knife cut a strip of the mid-rib on which is the vane of the feather; make 3 pieces, each 2 to 3 inches long.   White men glue these on to the arrow.   The Indians leave the mid-rib projecting at each end and by these lash the feathers without gluing.   The lashed feathers stand the weather better than those glued, but do not fly so well.   The Indians use sharp flint arrowheads for war and for big game, but for birds and small game they make arrowheads with a knob of hardwood or the knucklebone of some small animal.   The best arrowheads for our purpose are like the ferrule of an umbrella top; they receive the end of the shaft into them and keep it from splitting.

One of the best arrows I ever shot with was 28 inches long, 5-16 of an inch thick, had a ferrule head, and very small feathers.

The finishing touch of an arrow is " painting " it.   This is done for several purposes—first, to preserve it from damp which would twist the arrow and soften the glue that holds the feathers; second, each hunter paints all his arrows with his mark so as to know them; third, they are thus made bright-colored to help in finding them when lost.

There are four other things required by our archer—a smooth, hard arm-guard, or bracer, usually of hard leather.   The Indi-

CORRECT FORM IN SHOOTING
The diagram at bottom is to show the centres of heels in line with target

ans who use one make it of wood, grass or rawhide.   In photographs of famous Indians you may often see this on the left wrist, and will remember that it was there as a protection from the blow of the bow cord.   Some archers can shoot with the wrist bent so as to need no guard.   The three middle fingers of the right hand also need protection.   An old leather glove, with thumb and little finger cut away, will do very well for this, though the ready-made tips at the archery stores are more convenient. Some archers who practise all their lives can shoot without protecting the fingers.

The bow case and quiver are important. Any kind of a cover that will keep them from the rain, and hang on your back, will do, but there are many little things that help to make them handy. When the cover is off the arrows should project 3 or 4 inches so that they may be more easily drawn out. The Indians often carried very beautiful quivers of buckskin ornamented with quills and beads.

One day out West I saw an Omaha brave with a bow case and quiver covered with very odd material—a piece of common red and white cotton-print. When allowed to examine it, I felt some

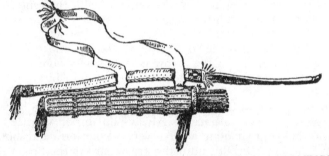

OMAHA BOW-CASE AND QUIVER OF BUCKSKIN AND QUILLWORK

other material underneath the print. After a little dickering he sold me bow, arrows, quiver, and all for a couple of dollars. I then ripped open the print and found my first suspicions confirmed; for underneath, the quiver was of buckskin, beautifully embroidered with red feathers and porcupine quills of deep red and turquoise blue. The Indian was as much puzzled by my preference for the quill-work as I was by his for the cotton-print.

The standard target, for men, is 4 feet across with a 9-inch bullseye, and around that 4 rings, each 4¾ inches wide. The bullseye counts 9, the other rings 7, 5, 3, 1. The bought targets are made of straw, but a good target may be made of a box filled with sods, or a bank covered with sacking on which are painted the usual rings.

Now comes the most important point of all—how to shoot.

There are several ways of holding an arrow, but only one good one. Most boys know the ordinary finger and thumb pinch, or grip. This is all very well for a toy bow, but a hunter's bow cannot be drawn that way. No one has strength enough in his fingers for it. The true archer's grip of the arrow is shown in the cut. The thumb and little finger have nothing to do with it.

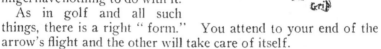

The Archer's Grip

As in golf and all such things, there is a right " form." You attend to your end of the arrow's flight and the other will take care of itself.

Stand perfectly straight. Plant your feet with the centres of the two heels in line with the target (cut page 119). Grasp the bow in the middle with the left hand and place the arrow on the string at the left side of the bow. Hold the bow plumb, and draw as above till the notch of the arrow is right under your eye and the head of the arrow back to the bow. The right elbow must be in the same line with the arrow. Let go the arrow by straightening the fingers a little, turning the hand outward at the bottom and drawing it back one inch. Always do this in exactly the same way and your shooting will be even. Your left hand should not move a hair's breadth until the arrow strikes the target.

To begin shooting put the target very near, within 15 or 20 yards, but the proper shooting distance when the archer is in good practice is 40 yards for a 4-foot target and 30 yards for a 3-foot target. A good shot, shooting 12 arrows at this, should score 50. When the archer has done it three times in succession—that is, scored 150 in 36 shots—it counts an honor. For high honor he should score 225 with 36 successive shots.

Long distance, or far shooting, is another test. To send an arrow 150 yards counts honor; 200 yards counts high honor.

The Indians generally used their bows at short range, so that it was easy to hit the mark. Rapid firing was important. In their archery competitions, therefore, the prize was given to the one who could have the most arrows in the air at once. Their record, according to Catlin, was 8. We reckon honor when we can have 5 in the air, and high honor for 7.

BUILDING A LOG-CABIN

(From *Country Life,* May, 1905)

There are as many different kinds of log-cabins as of any other architecture. It is best to begin with the simplest. The tools needed are a sharp axe, a crosscut saw, an inch auger, and a spade. It is possible to get along with nothing but an axe (many settlers had no other tool), but the spade, saw, and auger save much work.

For the site select a high, dry place, in or near the woods, and close to the drinking-water. It should be a sunny place, and with a view, preferably one facing south or east. Clear off and level the ground. Then bring your logs. These are more picturesque with the bark left on, but last longer peeled. Eight feet by twelve feet outside, makes a good cabin for three or four boys.

Cut and carry about twelve logs, each ten feet long and twelve more, each fourteen feet long. The logs should be at least six inches through. Soft wood is preferable, as it is easier to handle; the four ground logs, at least, should be of cedar, chestnut, or other wood that does not rot. Lay two of the fourteen-feet logs on the ground, at the places for the long sides, and seven feet apart. Then across them, at the end, lay two short ones, eleven feet apart. This leaves about a foot projecting from each log. Roll the last two into their resting-places, and flatten them till they sit firmly. It is of prime importance that each log rest immovably on the one below. Now cut the upper part of each end log, to an edge over each corner. (Fig. 1.)

Next put on two long logs, roll them on to the middle, taking care to change off, so the big end at a given corner may be followed next time by the small end, and insure the corner rising evenly. Roll one of these large logs close to where it is to be placed, then cut on its upper surface at each end a notch corresponding with the ridge on the log it is to ride on. When ready,

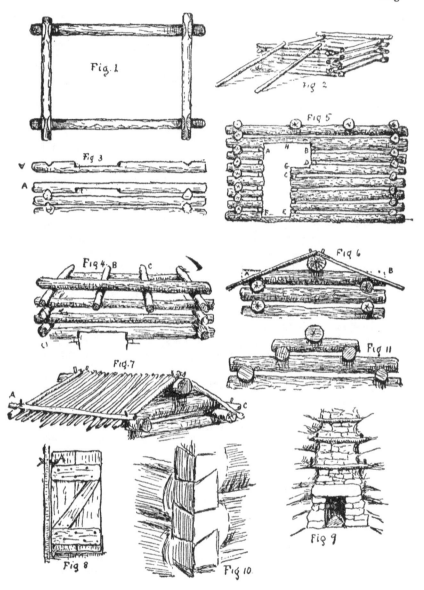

Fig. 1

Fig 2

Fig 5

Fig 3

Fig 4

Fig 6

Fig.7

Fig 11

Fig 8

Fig 10

Fig 9

half a roll drops it into place.   The log should be one to three inches above the one under it, and should not touch except at the ends.   Repeat the process now with the other sides, then the two ends, etc., *always keeping the line of the corner plumb*.   As the walls rise, it will be found necessary to *skid* the larger logs; that is, roll them up on two long logs, or skids, leaning against the wall.   (Fig. 2.)

When the logs are in place to the height of four and a half feet from the ground, it is time to decide where the door and window are to be, and at that place, while the next long log is lying on top, bottom up, cut out a piece four feet long and four inches deep.   Roll this into place.   (Fig. 3.)   One more log above this, or certainly two, will make your shanty high enough for boys.   Put on final end logs, then two others across the shanty.   (Fig. 4.)   Roll up the biggest, strongest log of all for the ridge (sometimes two are used side by side); it should lie along the middle of the four cross-pieces shown in Fig. 4.

The two cross-logs B and C, and the ridge-log should be very strong, as the roof is heavy.

Now we are ready to cut the doorway and window.

First, drive in blocks of wood between each of the logs, all the way down from A to the ground, and from B down to D, and C to E.   (Fig. 5.)   Saw down now from A halfway through the ground-log F.   Then from B down to halfway through the log D; now continue from G, cutting down to half through the ground-log.   Use the axe to split out the upper half of the ground-log, between the saw-cuts and also the upper half of the log D.

Hew a flat piece of soft wood, five or six inches wide, about two inches thick, and as long as the height of this doorway.   Set it up against the ends of the logs A to F.   Bore an auger-hole through it into the end of each log (these holes must not be in line lest they split the jamb), including the top and bottom ones, and drive into each a pin of oak.   This holds all safely.   Do the same on the other side, H to E, and put a small one down B, D, which is the side of the window.

Now we are ready to finish the roof.   Use the axe to bevel off the corners of the four cross-logs, A and B.   (Fig. 6.)   Then get a lot of strong poles, about five feet long, and lay them close

together along the two sides of the roof till it is covered with
poles; putting a very heavy one, or small log, on the outer edge
of each, and fastening it down with a pin into the ridge-log.
Cut two long poles and lay one on each of the lower ends of the
roof-poles, as at A, B, and C (Fig. 7), pinning them to the side
logs.

Cover this roof with a foot of hay or straw or grass, and cover
that again evenly with about four inches of stiff clay. Pack this
down. It will soon squeeze all that foot of straw down to little
more than one inch, and will make a warm and water-tight roof.

As the clay is very heavy, it is wise, before going inside, to test
the roof by jumping on it. If it gives too much, it will be well
to add a centre prop.

Now for the door. Hew out planks; two should be enough.
Fasten these together with two cross-pieces and one angle-piece,
using oak-pegs instead of nails, if you wish to be truly primitive.
For these the holes should be bored part way with a gimlet, and a
peg used larger than the hole. The lower end of the back plank
is left projecting in a point. (Fig. 8.) This point fits into a
hole pecked with a point or bored with auger into the door-
sill.

Bore another hole near the top of the door (A), and a corresponding one through the door-jamb between two logs. Set the
door in place. A strip of rawhide leather, a limber willow
branch, or a strip of hickory put through the auger-hole of the
door and wedged into the hole in the jamb, makes a truly wild-
wood hinge. A peg in the front jamb prevents the door going
too far out, and a string and peg inside answers for a latch.

The window-opening may be closed with a glass sash, with a
piece of muslin, or with the rawhide of an animal, scraped clear
of hair and stretched on a frame.

It now remains to chink and plaster the place.

Chinking is best done from the inside. Long triangular strips
and blocks of wood are driven in between the log and fastened
there with oak pins driven into the lower log till nothing but
small crannies remain. Some cabins are finished with moss
plugged into all the crannies, but mud worked into plaster does
better.

It should be put on the outside first, and afterwards finished from the inside. It is best done really with two plasterers working together, one inside and one out.

This completes the shanty, but a bunk and fireplace are usually added.

The fireplace may be in one corner, or in the middle of the end. It is easiest to make in the former.

Across the corner, peg three angle-braces, each about three feet long. These are to prevent the chimney falling forward.

Now begin to build with stone, using mud as mortar, a fireplace this shape. (Fig. 9.) Make the opening about eighteen inches across; carry it up two feet high, drawing it in a little, then lay a long stone across the front, after which build up the flue behind the corner-braces right up to the roof. The top corner-piece carries the rafter, that may be cut off to let the flue out. Build the chimney up outside as high as the highest part of the ridge.

But the ideal fireplace is made with the chimney on the *outside* of the cabin, at the middle of the end farthest from the door.

For this you must cut a hole in the end log, like a big, low window, pegging a jamb on the ends as before.

With stones and mud you now build a fireplace inside the shanty, with the big chimney carried up outside, always taking care that there are several inches of mud or stone between the fire and any of the logs.

In country where stone cannot be found, the fireplace is often built of mud, sustained by an outside cribbing of logs.

If the flue is fair size, that is, say, one-quarter the size of the fireplace opening, it will be sure to draw.

The bunk should be made before the chinks are plastered, as the hammering is apt to loosen the mud.

Cut eight or ten poles a foot longer than you need the bunk; cut the end of each into a flat board and drive these between the long logs at the right height and place for the bunk. Put a very big pole on the outer side, and all is ready for the bed; most woodmen make this of small fir boughs.

There are two other well-known ways of cornering the logs—one is simply flattening the logs where they touch. This, as well as the first one, is known in the backwoods of Canada as *hog-pen finish.* The really skilful woodsmen of the North always *dovetail* the corners and saw them flush. (Fig. 10.)

Sometimes it is desirable to make a higher gable than that which one ridge-log can make. Then it is made thus. (Fig. 11.)

This is as much slope as a clay roof should have; with any more, the clay would wash off.

This is the simplest way to build a log-cabin, but it illustrates all the main principles of log-building. Shingle roofs and gables; broad piazzas outside, and modern fitting inside, are often added nowadays in summer camp, but it must be clear that the more towny you make the cabin, the less woodsy it is, and less likely to be the complete rest and change that is desired.

For fuller instructions, see " Log-Cabins and Cottages," Wm. S. Wicks, 1900. (Pub. *Forest and Stream,* N. Y.) Also, " The Jack of All Trades," by Dan. C. Beard, Scribner's.

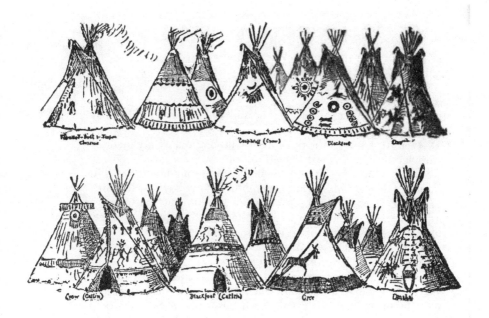

TEEPEES

(From *Ladies' Home Journal,* September, 1902)

Many famous campers have said that the Indian teepee is the best-known movable home. It is roomy, self-ventilating, cannot blow down, and is the only tent that admits of a fire inside.

Then why is it not everywhere used? Because of the difficulty of the poles. If on the prairie, you must carry your poles. If in the woods, you must cut them at each camp.

General Sibley, the famous Indian-fighter, invented a teepee with a single pole, and this is still used by our army. But it will not do for us. Its one pole is made in part of iron, and is very cumbersome as well as costly. The " Sibley " is ugly, too, compared with the real teepee, and if we are " playing Injun," not soldier, we shall stick to the famous and picturesque old teepee of the real Buffalo Indians.

In the " Buffalo days " this teepee was made of buffalo skin;

now it is made of some sort of canvas or cotton, but it is decorated much in the old style.

I tried to get an extra fine one made by the Indians especially as a model for our boys, but I found this no easy matter. I could not go among the Red-folk and order it as in a department store.

At length I solved the difficulty by buying one ready made from Thunder Bull, a chief of the Cheyennes.

It appears at the left end of the heading on page 128. This is a 20-foot teepee and is large enough for 10 boys to live in. A large one is easier to keep clear of smoke, but most boys will prefer a smaller one, as it is much handier, cheaper, and easier to make. I shall therefore give the working plan of a 10-foot teepee of the simplest form—the raw material of which can be bought new for less than $5.00.

It requires 22 square yards of 6- or 8-ounce duck, heavy unbleached muslin, or Canton flannel (the wider the better, as that saves labor in making up), which costs about $3.00; 100 feet of 3-16-inch clothesline, 25 cents; string for sewing rope ends, etc., 5 cents.

Of course, one can often pick up second-hand materials that are quite good and cost next to nothing. An old wagon cover, or two or three old sheets, will make the teepee, and even if they are patched it is all right; the Indian teepees are often mended where bullets and arrows have gone through them. Scraps of rope, if not rotted, will work in well enough.

Suppose you have new material to deal with. Get it machine run together 20 feet long and 10 feet wide. Lay this down perfectly flat (Cut I, p. 130). On a peg or nail at A in the middle of the long side put a 10-foot cord loosely, and then with a burnt stick in a loop at the other end draw the half-circle B C D. Now mark out the two little triangles at A. A E is 6 inches, A F and E F each one foot; the other triangle, A R G, is the same size. Cut the canvas along these dotted lines. From the scraps left over cut two pieces for smoke-flaps, as shown. On the long corner of each (H in No. 1, I in No. 2) a small three-cornered piece should be sewed, to make a pocket for the end of the pole.

Now sew the smoke-flaps to the cover so that M L of No. 1 is neatly fitted to P E, and N O of No. 2 to Q G.

Pattern of 10-Foot Teepee.

The Complete Teepee Cover — Unornamented.
A — Frame for Door.
B — Door Completed.

Two inches from the edge B P make a double row of holes; each hole is 1½ inches from its mate, and each pair is 5 inches from the next pair, except at the 2-foot space marked " door," where no holes are needed.

The holes on the other side, Q D, must exactly fit on these.

At A fasten very strongly a 4-foot rope by the middle. Fasten the end of a 10-foot cord to J and another to K; hem a rope all along in the bottom, B C D. Cut 12 pieces of rope each about 15 inches long, fasten one firmly to the canvas at B, another at the point D, and the rest at regular distances to the hem rope along the edge between, for peg loops. The teepee cover is now made.

For the door (some never use one) take a limber sapling ¾-inch thick and 5½ feet long, also one 22 inches long. Bend the long one into a horseshoe and fasten the short one across the ends (A on p. 130, lower figure). On this stretch canvas, leaving a flap at the top in the middle of which two small holes are made (B, p. 130), so as to hang the door on a lacing-pin. Nine of these lacing-pins are needed. They are of smooth, round, straight, hard wood, a foot long and ¼-inch thick. Their way of skewering the two edges together is seen in the Omaha teepee at the end of the line.

Twelve poles also are needed. They should be as straight and smooth as possible; crooked, rough poles are signs of a bad house-keeper—a squaw is known by her teepee poles. They should be 13 or 14 feet long and about 1½ inches thick at the top. Two are for the smoke-vent; they may be more slender than the others. Last of all, make a dozen stout short pegs about 15 inches long and about 1½ inches thick. Now all the necessary parts of the teepee are made.

This is how the Indian tent is put up: Tie 3 poles together at a point about 2 feet higher than the canvas, spread them out in a tripod the right distance apart; then lay the other poles (except 3, including the 2 slender ones) in the angles, their lower ends forming the proper circle. Bind them all with a rope, letting its end hang down inside for an anchor. Now fasten the 2 ropes at A to the stout pole left over at a point 10 feet up. Raise this into its place, and the teepee cover with it, opposite where the door is to be. Carry the two wings of the tent around till they overlap and fasten together with the lacing-pins. Put the end of a vent-pole in each of the vent flap pockets, outside of the teepee. Peg down the edges of the canvas at each loop if a storm is coming, otherwise a few will do. Hang the door on a convenient lacing-pin.

Drive a stout stake inside the teepee, tie the anchor rope to this and the teepee is ready for weather.   In the centre dig a hole 18 inches wide and 6 inches deep for the fire.

The fire is the great advantage of the teepee, and the smoke the great disadvantage, but experience will show how to manage this.   Keep the smoke-vent swung down wind, or at least quartering down.   Sometimes you must leave the door a little open or raise the bottom of the teepee cover a little on the windward side. If this makes too much draft on your back, stretch a piece of canvas between two or three of the poles inside the teepee, in front of the opening made and reaching to the ground.   The draft will go up behind this.

By these tricks you can make the vent draw the smoke.   But after all the main thing is to use only the best and dryest of wood. This makes a clear fire.   There will always be more or less smoke 7 or 8 feet up, but it worries no one there and keeps the mosquitoes away.

You should always be ready for a storm over-night.   You must study the wind continually and be weatherwise—that is, a woodcrafter—if you are to make a success of the teepee.

And remember this: The Indians did not look for hardships. They took care of their health so as to withstand hardship when it came, but they made themselves as comfortable as possible.   They never slept on the ground if they could help it. Catlin tells us of the beautiful 4-post beds the Mandans used to make in their lodges.   The Blackfeet make neat beds of willow rods carefully peeled, and the Eastern Indians cut piles of pine and fir branches to keep them off the ground.

Another thing of importance: Catlin says that the real wild Indians were " cleanly."   They became " filthy " when half civilized.   Cleanliness around the camp should be a law.   When I camp, even in the Rockies, I aim to leave the ground as undefiled as when I came.   I always dig a hole or several if need be, and say : " Now, boys, I want all tins and rubbish put here and buried. I want this place left as clean as we found it."   This may be a matter of sentiment in the Western mountains, but in the woods near home you will find you will win many friends if you enforce the law of cleanliness.

Near the end of the row above is Gray-Wolf's teepee.   I came across this on the Upper Missouri in 1897. It was the most brilliant affair I ever saw on the Plains, for on the bright red ground of the canvas were his totems and medicine, in yellow, blue, green, and black. The day I sketched it a company of United States soldiers under orders had forcibly taken away his two children "to send them to school, according to law"; so Gray-Wolf was going off at once, without pitching his tent. His little daughter, "The Fawn," looked at me with fear, thinking I was coming to drag her off to school. I coaxed her, then gave her a quarter. She smiled, because she knew it would buy sweetmeats.

Then I said: "Little Fawn, run and tell your father that I am his friend, and I want to see his great red teepee."

"The Fawn" came back and said, "My father hates you."

"Tell your mother that I will pay her if she will put up the teepee."

"The Fawn" went to her mother, and, improving my offer, told her that "that white man will give much money to see the red teepee up."

The squaw looked out. I held up a dollar and got only a sour look, but another squaw appeared. After some haggling they agreed to put up the teepee for $3.00. The poles were already standing. They unrolled the great cloth and deftly put it up in less than 20 minutes, but did not try to put down the anchor rope, as the ground was too hard to drive a stake into.

My sketch was half finished when the elder woman called the younger and pointed westward. They chattered together a moment and then proceeded to take down the teepee. I objected. They pointed angrily toward the west and went on. I protested that I had paid for the right to make the sketch; but in spite of me the younger squaw scrambled like a monkey up the front pole, drew the lacing-pins, and the teepee was down and rolled up in ten minutes.

I could not understand the pointing to the west, but five minutes after the teepee was down a dark spot appeared; this became a cloud and in a short time we were in the midst of a wind-storm that threw down all teepees that were without the anchor rope, and certainly the red teepee would have been one of those to suffer but for the sight and foresight of the old Indian woman.

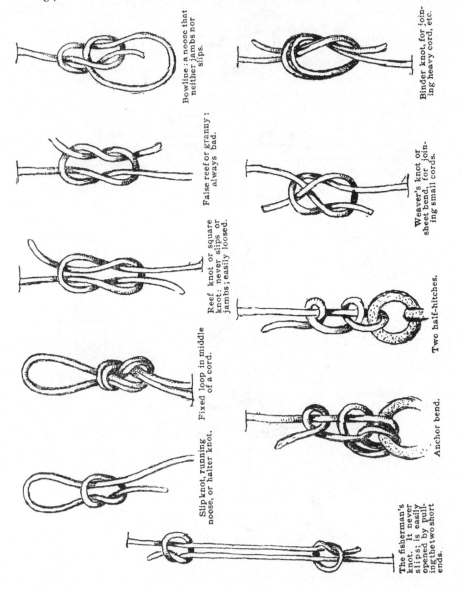

Bowline: a noose that neither jambs nor slips.

Binder knot, for joining heavy cord, etc.

False reef or granny: always bad.

Weaver's knot or sheet bend, for joining small cords.

Reef knot or square knot: never slips or jambs; easily loosed.

Fixed loop in middle of a cord.

Two half-hitches.

Slip knot, running noose, or halter knot.

Anchor bend.

The fisherman's knot. It never slips; is easily opened by pulling the two short ends.

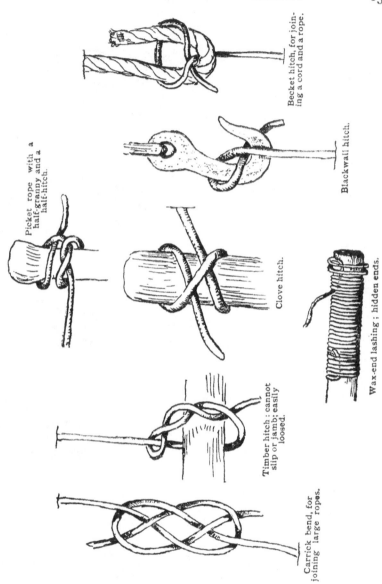

Becket hitch, for joining a cord and a rope.

Blackwall hitch.

Picket rope with a half-granny and a half-hitch.

Clove hitch.

Wax-end lashing; hidden ends.

Timber hitch: cannot slip or jamb; easily loosed.

Carrick bend, for joining large ropes.

TRACKING OR TRAILING

Uppermost,
well-devel-
oped human
foot.

Middle, a
foot always
cramped by
boots.

Bottom, a
bare foot,
never in
boots.

Dog tracks,
Front and back.
(½ life-size.)

Cat tracks,
front and back.
(½ life-size.)

Muskrat tracks.
(⅓ life-size.)

The first step in tracking or trailing is learning the footmarks of each of the common animals. A number of these are given now. A more elaborate article on the Secrets of the Trail will appear in a subsequent issue.

TRACKS

1. Blarina in snow.
2. Deermouse.

3. Meadowmouse.
4. Masked shrew.

Wild Turkey.　　　　Toad.　　　　Crow.

TRACKS

1. Jackrabbit.　2. Cottontail.　3. Gray squirrel.　4. Coon.　5. Ground-bird, such as
Quail　6. Tree-bird.　7. A bird living partly in tree, partly on ground.

AMERICAN DIALECTS

To tell what State a man comes from (except he be much travelled) :—

If from the South, he says " A " for " I " and " Sah for " Sir."

If from the Gulf States, " Cahline " for " Carolina." Only certain Europeans say " Caroleena."

If from the Ohio Valley, he says " Cincinnatah " for " Cincinnati."

If from the Middle West, he says " Mizzoura " for " Missouri."

If from the Northwest, he says " Montanna " for " Montana."

If from Boston, or south of Mason and Dixon's line, he says " maw-ning " for " morning."

If from any northern place but Boston, he rolls the " R " and says " morrrning."

If from the Northern Rockies, he says " Coloray-do " for " Colorado."

If from California, he says " Frisco " for " San Francisco."

If from Los Angeles, he makes the " g " hard; otherwise, soft.

If from Texas or Arizona, he calls " Rio Grande " " Reeo Gran-day "; elsewhere, " Ry-o Grand."

If from Georgia, he calls it " Jo-ja."

If from Maryland or the mountains of New England, he says " me-ountan " for " mountain."

If from St. Louis, he calls it " Saint Lou-is "; elsewhere " Saint Lou-ee."

If from Louisiana, he says " Noo Or'-lens "; elsewhere " New Or-le'ans."

If from Chicago, he says " hef " for " half " and " kef " for " calf."

If from Canada, he calls " Toronto " " Tranto."

If from Montreal, he calls it " Monreal."

PART IV. THE GAMES

DEER-HUNTING

The Deer Hunt has proved one of our most successful games.

The deer is a dummy, best made with a wire frame, on which soft hay is wrapped till it is of proper size and shape, then all is covered with open burlap. A few touches of white and black make it very realistic.

If time does not admit of a well-finished deer, one can be made of a sack stuffed with hay, decorated at one end with a smaller sack for head and neck, and set on four thin sticks.

The side of the deer is marked with a large oval, and over the heart is a smaller one.

Bows and arrows only are used to shoot this deer.

A pocketful of corn, peas, or other large grain is now needed for scent. The boy who is the deer for the first hunt takes the dummy under his arm and runs off, getting ten minutes' start, or until he comes back and shouts "ready!" He leaves a trail of corn, dropping two or three grains for every yard and making the trail as crooked as he likes, playing such tricks as a deer would do to baffle his pursuers. Then he hides the deer in any place he fancies, but not among rocks or on the top of a ridge, because in one case many arrows would be broken, and in the other, lost.

Wooden legged Deer

The hunters now hunt for this deer just as for a real deer, either following the trail or watching the woods ahead; the best hunters combine the two.   If at any time the trail is quite lost the one in charge shouts "*Lost Trail!*" After that the one who finds the trail scores *two*. Any one giving a false alarm by shouting "*Deer*" is fined *five*.

Thus they go till some one finds the deer. He shouts "*Deer!*" and scores *ten* for finding it. The others shout "*Second,*" "*Third,*" etc., in order of seeing it, but they do not score.

The finder must shoot at the deer with his bow and arrow from the very spot whence he saw it. If he misses, the second hunter may step up five paces, and have his shot. If *he* misses,

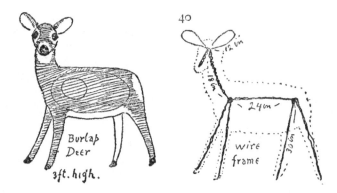

the third one goes five, and so on till some one hits the deer, or until the ten-yard limit is reached. If the finder is within ten yards on sighting the deer, and misses his shot, the other hunters go back to the ten-yard limit. Once the deer is hit, all the shooting must be from the exact spot whence the successful shot was fired.

A shot in the big oval is a *body wound;* that scores *five.* A shot outside that is a *scratch;* that scores *two.* A shot in the small oval or heart is a *heart wound;* it scores *ten,* and ends the hunt. Arrows which do not stick do not count, unless it can be proved that they passed right through, in which case they take the highest score that they pierced.

If all the arrows are used, and none in the heart, the deer escapes, and the boy who was deer scores *twenty-five.*

The one who found the dummy is deer for the next hunt. A clever deer can add greatly to the excitement of the game.

Originally we used paper for scent, but found it bad. It littered the woods, yesterday's trail was confused with that of to-day, etc. Corn proved better, because the birds and the squirrels kept it cleaned up from day to day, and thus the ground was always ready for a fresh start.   But the best of all is the hoof mark for the shoe.   These iron hoof-marks are fast to a pair of shoes, and leave a trail much like a real deer.   This has several advantages.   It gives the hunter a chance to tell where the trail doubled, and which way the deer was going.   It is more realistic, and a boy who can follow this skilfully can follow a living deer. In actual practice it is found well to use a little corn with this on

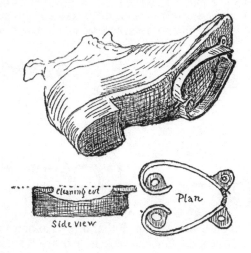

Side view   Cleaning cut   Plan

the hard places, a plan quite consistent with realism, as every hunter will recall.

It is strictly forbidden to any hunter to stand in front of the firing line; all must be back of the line on which the shooter stands.

There is no limit to the situations and curious combinations in this hunt.   The deer may be left standing or lying.   There is no law why it should not be hidden behind a solid tree trunk.   The game develops as one follows it.   After it has been played for some time with the iron hoof-mark as above the boys grow so skilful on the trail that we can dispense with even the corn. The iron mark like a deer hoof leaves a very realistic "slot" or track, which the more skilful boys readily follow through the woods. A hunt is usually for three, five or more deer, according to agreement, and the result is reckoned by points on the whole chase.

THE BEAR HUNT

This is played by half a dozen or more boys. Each has a club about the size and shape of a baseball club, but made of *straw* tied around two or three switches and tightly sewn up in burlap.

One big fellow is selected for the bear. He has a school-bag

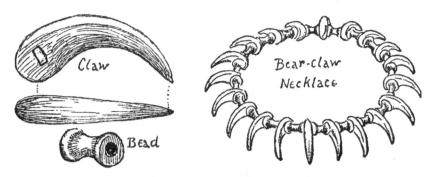

tightly strapped on his back, and in that a toy balloon fully blown up. This is his heart. On his neck is a bear-claw necklace of wooden beads and claws. (See cut.)

He has three dens about one hundred yards apart in a triangle. While in his den the bear is safe. If the den is a tree or rock, he is safe while touching it. He is obliged to come out when the

Straw Club

chief hunter counts 100, and must go the rounds of the three till the hunt is settled.

The object of the hunters is to break the balloon or heart, that is, kill the bear. He must drop dead when the heart bursts. The hunter who kills him claims the necklace.

But the bear also has a club for defence. Each hunter must wear a hat, and once the bear knocks a hunter's hat off, *that one is dead* and out of this hunt. He must drop where his hat falls.

Tackling of any kind is forbidden.

The bear wins by killing or putting to flight all the hunters. In this case he keeps the necklace.

The savageness of these big bears is indescribable. Many lives are lost in each hunt, and it has several times happened that the whole party of hunters has been exterminated by some monster of unusual ferocity.

This game has also been developed into a play.

SPEARING THE GREAT STURGEON

This water game is exceedingly popular and is especially good for public exhibition, being spectacular and full of amusement and excitement.

The outfit needed is :—

(1) A sturgeon roughly formed of soft wood; it should be about four feet long and nearly a foot thick at the head. It may be made realistic, or a small log pointed at both ends will serve.

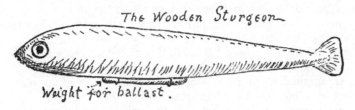

The Wooden Sturgeon

Weight for ballast.

(2) Two spears with six-inch steel heads and wooden handles (about four feet long). The points should be sharp, but not the barbs. Sometimes the barbs are omitted altogether. Each head should have an eye to which is attached twenty feet of one-quarter inch rope. On each rope, six feet from the spearhead, is a fathom-mark made by tying on a rag or cord.

(3) Two boats with crews. Each crew consists of a spear-

man, who is captain, and one or two oarsmen or paddlers, of which the after one is the pilot. All should be expert swimmers or else wear life-belts during the game.

The Game. Each boat has a base or harbor; this is usually part of the shore opposite that of the enemy; or it obviates all danger of collision if the boats start from the same side. The sturgeon is left by the referee's canoe at a point midway between the bases. At the word "Go!" each boat leaves its

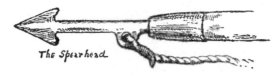

The Spearhead

base and, making for the sturgeon, tries to spear it, then drag it by the line to his base. When both get their spears into it the contest becomes a tug of war until one of the spears pulls out.

The sturgeon is landed when the prow of the boat that has it in tow touches its proper base, even though the spear of the enemy is then in the fish: or it is landed when the fish itself touches base. The boats change bases after each heat.

Matches are usually for one, three, or five sturgeon. Points are counted only for the landing of the fish, but the referee may give the decision on a foul or a succession of fouls, or the delinquent may be set back one or more boat-lengths.

Sometimes the game is played in canoes or boats, with one man as spearman and crew.

Rules. It *is not allowed* to push the sturgeon into a new position with the spear or paddle before striking.

It *is allowed* to pull the sturgeon under the boat or pass it around by using the line after spearing.

It *is allowed* to lay hands on the other boat to prevent a collision, but otherwise it is forbidden to touch the other boat or crew or paddle or spear or line, or to lay hands on the fish, or to touch it with the paddle or oar, or touch your own spear while it is in the fish, or to tie the line around the fish except so far as this may be accidentally done in spearing.

It *is allowed* to dislodge the enemy's spear by throwing your own over it. The purpose of the barbs is to assist in this.

It is allowed to run onto the sturgeon with the boat.

It *is absolutely forbidden to throw the spear over the other boat or over the heads of your crew.*

In towing the sturgeon the fathom-mark must be over the gunwale—at least six feet of line should be out when the fish is in tow. It is not a foul to have less, but the spearman must at once let it out if the umpire or the other crew cries " fathom!"

The spearman is allowed to drop the spear and use the paddle or oar at will, but not to resign his spear to another of the crew. The spearman must be in his boat when the spear is thrown.

If the boat is upset the referee's canoe helps them to right.

Each crew must accept the backset of its accidents.

TILTING IN THE WATER

For this we usually have two boats or war canoes manned by four men each. These are a spearman, who is also a captain, a pilot, and two oarsmen.

Head of Tilting Spear.

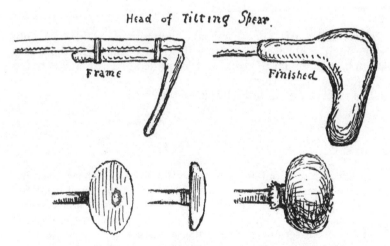

Frame   Finished

The spearman is armed with a light pole or bamboo 8 or 10 feet long, with a soft pad on the end. Sometimes this is further provided with a hook. This is a forked branch with limbs a foot long; one is lashed to the bamboo, the other projecting out a foot, and slightly backward. The end of the spear and the fork are now thoroughly padded with burlap to the shape of a duck's head and bill. And it must be cased in waterproof, to keep it from getting wet and heavy. The object of the hook is to change suddenly from pushing, and to pull the enemy by hooking round his neck. Each boat should have a quarterdeck or raised platform at one end, on which the spearman stands.

The battle is fought in rounds and by points.

To put your opponent back into the canoe with one foot counts you 5; two feet, 10. If he loses his spear you count 5 (excepting when he is put overboard). If you put him down on one knee on the fighting deck, you count 5; two knees, 10. If you put him overboard it counts 25. One hundred points is a round.

A battle is for one or more rounds, as agreed on.

It is forbidden to hook or strike below the belt.

The umpire may dock for fouls.

CANOE TAG

Any number of canoes or boats may engage in this. A rubber cushion, a hot-water bag full of air, any rubber football, or a cotton bag with a lot of corks in it, is needed. The game is to tag the other canoe by throwing this *into* it.

The rules are as in ordinary cross-tag.

SCOUTING

Scouts are sent out in pairs or singly. A number of points are marked on the map at equal distances from camp, and the scouts draw straws to see who goes where. If one place is obviously hard, the scout is allowed a fair number of points as handicap. All set out at same time, go direct, and return as soon as possible.

Points are thus allowed :—

Last back, *zero* for travelling.

The others count one for each minute they are ahead of the last.

Points up to 100 are allowed for their story on return.

Sometimes we allow 10 points for each Turtle they have seen; 10 for each Owl seen and properly named; 5 for each Hawk, and 1 each for other wild birds; also 2 for a Cat; 1 for a Dog.

No information is given the scout; he is told to go to such a point and do so and so, but is fined points if he hesitates or asks how or why, etc.

THE GAME OF QUICKSIGHT

Make two boards about a foot square, divide each into twenty-five squares; get ten nuts and ten pebbles. Give to one player one board, five nuts, and five pebbles. He places these on the squares in any pattern he fancies, and when ready the other player is allowed to see it for five seconds. Then it is covered up, and from the memory of what he saw the second player must re-

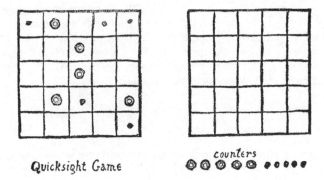

Quicksight Game

counters

produce the pattern on his own board. He counts one for each that was right, and takes off one for each that was wrong. They take turn and turn about.

This game is a wonderful developer of the power to see and memorize quickly.

FAR-SIGHT, OR SPOT-THE-RABBIT

Take two six-inch squares of stiff white pasteboard or whitened wood. On each of these draw an outline Rabbit, one an exact duplicate of the other. Make twenty round black wafers or spots, each half an inch across. Let one player stick a few of these on

6 inches sq

one Rabbit-board and set it up in full light. The other, beginning at 100 yards, draws near till he can see the spots well enough to reproduce the pattern on the other which he carries. If he can do it at 75 yards he has wonderful eyes. Down even to 70 (done 3 times out of 5) he counts high honor; from 70 to 60 counts honor. Below that does not count at all.

POLE-STAR

Each competitor is given a long, straight stick, in daytime, and told to lay it due north and south. In doing this he may guide himself by sun, moss, or anything he can find in nature,—anything, indeed, except a compass.

The direction is checked by a good compass corrected for the locality. The one who comes nearest wins.

It is optional with the judges whether the use of a time-piece is to be allowed.

RABBIT HUNT

The game of Rabbit-hunting is suited for two hunters in limited grounds.

Three little sacks of brown burlap, each about eight inches by twelve, are stuffed with hay.

At any given place in the woods the two hunters stand in a ten-foot circle with their bows and arrows. One boy is blind-folded; the other, without leaving the circle, throws the Rabbits into good hiding-places on the ground. Then the second hunter has to find the Rabbits and shoot them without leaving the circle. The lowest number of points wins, as in golf. If the hunter has to leave the circle he gets one point for every step he takes outside. After he sees the Rabbit he must keep to that spot and shoot till it is hit once. One shot kills it, no matter where struck. For every shot he misses he gets five points.

After his first shot at each Rabbit the hider takes alternate shots with him.

If it is the hider who kills the Rabbit, the hunter adds ten points to his score. If the hunter hits it, he takes ten off his score.

If the hunter fails to find all the Rabbits, he scores twenty-five for each one he gives up.

The hider cannot score at all. He can only help his friend into trouble. Next time the two change places.

A match is usually for two brace of Rabbits.

HOSTILE SPY

Hanging from the totem pole is a red or yellow horsetail. This is the Grand Medicine Scalp of the band. The Hostile Spy has to steal it. The leader goes around on the morning of the day and whispers to the various braves, " Look out— there's a spy in camp." At length he gets secretly near the one he has selected for spy and whispers, " Look out, there's a spy in camp, and *you are it.*" He gives him at the same time some bright-colored badge, that he must wear as soon as he has secured the Medicine Scalp. He must not hide the scalp on his person, but keep it in view.   He has all day till sunset to get away with it.   If he gets across the river or other limit, with warriors in close pursuit, they give him ten arrow-heads (two and one-half cents each), or other ransom agreed on.   If he gets away safely and hides it, he can come back and claim fifteen arrowheads from the Council as ransom for the scalp.   If he is caught, he pays his captor ten arrow-heads ransom for his life.

THE MAN-HUNT

This is played with a Scout and ten or more Hostiles, or hounds, according to the country, more when it is rough or wooded.

The Scout is given a letter addressed to the " Military Commandant " * of any given place a mile or two away.   He is told to take the letter to any one of three given houses, and get it endorsed, with the hour when he arrived, then return to the starting-point within a certain time.

The Hostiles are sent to a point halfway, and let go by a starter at the *same time* as the Scout leaves the camp.   They are to intercept him.

If they catch him before he delivers the letter he must ransom his life by paying each two arrow-heads (or other forfeit) and his captor keeps the letter as a trophy.   If he gets through, but is caught on the road back, he pays half as much for his life.   If he gets through, but is over time, it is a draw.   If he gets through successfully on time he claims three arrow-heads from each Hostile and keeps the letter as a trophy.

They may not follow him into the house (that is, the Fort), but may surround it at one hundred yards distance.   They do not know which three houses he is free to enter, but they do know that these are within certain narrow limits.

The Scout should wear a conspicuous badge (hat, shirt, coat, or feather), and may ride a wheel or go in a wagon, etc., as long as his badge is clearly visible.

---

* The " Military Commandant " is usually the lady of the house that he gets to.

To " tag " the Scout is not to capture. " The blockade to be binding must be effectual."

HUNT THE COON

This is an indoor game, founded on the familiar " Hunt the Thimble."

We use a little dummy coon; either make it or turn a ready-made toy rabbit into one by adding tail and black mask, and cropping the ears.

All the players but one go out of the room. That one places the coon anywhere in sight, high or low, but in plain view; all come in and seek. The first to find it, sits down silently, and scores 1. Each sits down, on seeing it, giving no clue to the others.

The first to score 3 coons is winner, usually. Sometimes we play till every one but one has a coon; that one is the booby. The others are first, second, etc.

Sometimes each is given his number in order of finding it. Then, after 7 or 8 coons, these numbers are added up, and the *lowest* is winner.

SPEAR-FIGHTS

This is an indoor game with outdoor weapons. The soft-headed, 8-foot spears of the tilting-match are used. The contestants stand on a 3-foot circle, 8 feet apart. Each tries to put the other off his circle. One foot off counts 1; both feet off counts 2 for the other party. Barrels are better than circles to stand on.

Games are for 7, 11, or 13 points.

NAVAJO FEATHER-DANCE

An eagle feather hung on a horse-hair, so as to stand upright, is worked by a hidden operator, so as to dance and caper. The dancer has to imitate all its motions. A marionette may be used. It is a great fun-maker.

FEATHER FOOTBALL OR FEATHER-BLOW

This is an indoor, wet-weather game.

The players hold a blanket on the knees or on the table. A soft feather is put in the middle. As many may play as can get near. They may be in sides, 2 or 4, or each for himself. At the signal " Go! " each tries to blow the feather off the blanket at the enemy's side, and so count one for himself.

A game is usually best out of 7, 11, or 13.

COCK-FIGHTING

Make 2 stout sticks, each 2 feet long (broom sticks will do). Pad each of these on the end with a ball of rag. These are the spurs. Make an 8-foot ring. The two rivals are on their hunkers, each with a stick through behind his knees, his hands clasped in front of the knees, and the arms under the ends of the spurs.

Now they close; each aiming to upset the other; to make him lose his spurs or to put him out of the ring, any of which ends that round, and scores 1 for the victor. If both fall, or lose a spur, or go out together, it is a draw. Battle is for 7, 11, or 13 rounds.

HAND-WRESTLING

This is a Ju-Jitsu game, introduced by Dr. L. H. Gulick.

The two contestants stand right toe to right toe, each right hand clasped; left feet braced; left hand free. At the word " Go! " each tries to unbalance the other: that is, make him lift or move one of his feet. A lift or a shift ends the round.

Battles are for best out of 5, 7, 11, or 13 rounds.

BADGER-PULLING

The two contestants, on hands and knees, face each other. A strong belt or strap is buckled into one great loop that passes

round the head of each: that is, crosses his nape. Halfway between them is a dead line. The one who pulls the other over this
line is winner.

The contestant can at any time end the bout by lowering his
head so the strap slips off; but this counts 1 against him.

Game is best out of 5, 7, 11, or 13 points.

POISON

This is an ancient game. A circle about 3 feet across is
drawn on the ground. The players, holding hands, make a ring
around this, and try to make one of the number step into the
poison circle. He can evade it by side-stepping, by jumping over,
or by dragging another fellow into it.

First to make the misstep is " it " for the time or for next game.

HAT-BALL

When I was among the Chepewyan Indians of Great Slave
Lake, in 1907, I made myself popular with the young men, as
well as boys, by teaching them the old game of hat-ball.

The players (about a dozen) put their hats in a row near a
house, fence, or log (hollows up). A dead line is drawn 10 feet
from the hats; all must stand outside of that. The one who
is " it " begins by throwing a soft ball into one of the hats. If
he misses the hat, a chip is put into his own, and he tries over.
As soon as he drops the ball into a hat, the owner runs to get
the ball; all the rest run away. The owner must not follow beyond the dead line, but must throw the ball at some one. If he
hits him, a chip goes into that person's hat; if not, a chip goes
into his own.

As soon as some one has 5 chips, he wins the booby prize: that
is, he must hold his hand out steady against the wall, and each
player has 5 shots at it with the ball, as he stands on the dead-line.

DUCK-ON-A-ROCK

This is a good, old grandfather game.

Each player has a large, smooth, roundish stone, about 5 or

6 inches through. This is his duck. He keeps it permanently.

The rock is any low boulder, block, stump, bump, or hillock on level ground. A dead-line is drawn through the rock, and another parallel, 15 feet away, for a firing-line.

The fellow who is " it," or " keeper," perches his duck on the rock. The others stand at the firing-line and throw their ducks at his. They must not pick them up or touch them with their hands when they are beyond the dead-line. If one does, then the keeper can tag him (unless he reaches the firing-line), and send him to do duty as keeper at the rock.

But they can coax their ducks with their feet, up to the dead line, not beyond, then watch for a chance to dodge back to the firing-line, where they are safe at all times.

If the duck is knocked off by any one in fair firing, the keeper is powerless till he has replaced it. Meantime, most of the players have secured their ducks and got back safe to the firing-line.

ROADSIDE CRIBBAGE

This is a game we often play in the train, to pass the time pleasantly.

Sometimes one party takes the right side of the road, with the windows there, and the other the left. Sometimes all players sit on the same side.

The game is, whoever is first to see certain things agreed on, scores so many points. Thus:

A Crow or a Cow counts.............. 1
A Horse............................. 2
A Sheep............................. 3
A Goat.............................. 4
A Cat............................... 5
A Hawk.............................. 6
An Owl.............................. 7

The winner is the one who first gets 25 or 50 points, as agreed.

When afoot, one naturally takes other things for points, as certain trees, flowers, etc.

Many good camp games will be found in Dan C. Beard's " Boy Pioneers " (Scribner's, 1909).

THE WAR DANCE

By Ernest Thompson Seton

Each brave selects a squaw for this. Ten to thirty couples take part. They come out of the woods in procession, singing the Omaha tribal prayer (see Fletcher, p. 29). They sit in a large circle, alternately brave and squaw. In the centre is a block with a scalp on it (these may be left out). Each squaw has a club by her side.

Squaws begin to sing the *Coona* song (*Cahuilla Bird Dance Song—Wawan Press*) or *Omaha Love Song* (p. 50, Fletcher), guided by Medicine-man and drum. At length the song stops.

Squaws begin nudging the braves and pointing to the scalp-block. New music by the Medicine-man begins. The Zonzi-mondi or other dance song.* The braves jump up, dance around once, with heads high in air, almost held backward and not crouching at all. (*They carry no clubs yet.*)

After going once around, each is back again near his squaw,

---

* The song most used is the Moccasin Song, thus:

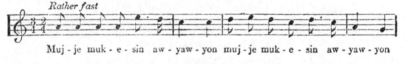

Muj - je muk - e - sin aw - yaw - yon muj - je muk - e - sin aw - yaw - yon

muj - je muk - e - sin aw - yaw - yon muj - je muk - e - sin aw - yaw - yon

This is from Fred R. Burton's " Primitive American Music," 1909.

There are many fine airs and dances in Alice C. Fletcher's " Indian Story and Song," Small, Maynard & Co., 1900. ($1.00.)

and she holds out to him the war-club and utters the little squaw-yelp. Each brave takes his club, and now begins the crouch dance. Going three times around, and each time crouching lower while the squaws stand or sit in a circle, arms down tight to side, but bodies swaying in time to music. In the fourth round all are crouching very low and moving sideways, facing inward.

The music suddenly changes, and all do the slow sneak toward the centre with much pantomime and keeping right foot advanced always. The squaws watch eagerly and silently, leaning forward, shading their eyes with one hand. All the braves strike the scalp-block together, utter the loud war-whoop, and stand for a moment with hands and weapons raised high, then in time to the fast drum, dance quickly erect with high steps and high heads to the squaws, who utter the squaw-yelp for welcome, and all sit down as before.

The squaws begin the singing again, repeat the whole scene, but this time the chief falls when the block is struck, and is left lying there when the other braves retire.

His squaw stands up, and says: " Where is my chief who led you to battle? Why has he not come back to me?"

All look and whisper; the squaws get up to seek. At once they find him, and, kneeling about him with clasped hands, break forth in the squaw-lament for the dead, which is a high-pitched, quavering wail. The warriors lift him up and slowly carry him off the scene, out of sight, followed by the squaws, who, with heads bent, sing:

(Air: Bark Canoe. See Burton's Book.)

> Our chief, our warrior true
> Is lost to all, to me and you.
> Dire fall our vengeance due
> On those who slew our warrior true.

Repeat it many times; as they disappear, the music dies away, fainter and fainter.

If no squaws take part, let the braves enter in procession, singing, and carry their clubs throughout, and seek the dead as the squaws do.

THE FIRE-FLY DANCE

By Ernest Thompson Seton, 1906

This should be played in an open space at night, or late enough in the evening to insure a dim light.

The fire-flies are ten to thirty children in any costume, each bearing a stick that is afire, but not blazing. If played indoors, dim little candle-lamps on sticks could be used, and in any case out of doors it would be well to have prepared torches of fire-holding punk which can be bought of fireworks dealers, or made by soaking rotten wood in saltpetre solution. This can be carried in a split stick. In some cases electric lamps might serve.

The fire-flies come in, making many dazzling and beautiful figures of fire. They dance and evolute, waving their torches. A good figure is made by all standing in a circle and each revolving his torch overhead in an upright circle; another, by every other one zigzagging it up and down like lightning. The best singer stands in the centre and sings.

(Air: Jingle-bells)

We are the merry Fire-flies,
    A-glinting through the trees.
We pirouette in gloomy spots,
    Or skate upon the breeze.

(All join in Chorus)

Chorus.   Twinkle, twinkle, twinkle, glancing,
    Sleepy all the day,
But with shade of night advancing
    Comes our time to play.

158

We haven't got a single care,
    We twinkle all the night,
And each one does his little best
    To fill his world with light.

(Chorus)

We never heard of enemies,
    From every fear we're free,
And the blacker that the night is
    The better pleased are we.

(Chorus)

(Now an Owl appears. A blanket draped across the arms will do for wings, and, aided by a mask, is sufficient make-up. He comes swooping and hooting into the ring. The Fire-flies open, but close about him dancing and singing:)

The merriest time of day is night,
    And merriest kind of fowl,
If everything on earth were right,
    Would be, of course, the Owl.

(The Owl hoots and hisses angrily. They laugh and shout in glee:)

(Chorus)

Oh, hear him try to frighten us
    That never knew a fear,
And if he'll neither dance nor sing
    We'll chase him out of here.

(They flash their torches in his face and he flies away, hooting and shrieking.)

(Chorus)

(A very big Bear now comes blundering in. The Fire-flies flash around him singing:)

Ho, shaggy, surly, burly Bear!
  So pleased you came to-night.
Come, dance among the trees with us,
  'Twill make a pretty sight.

(The Bear starts back and growls.)

(Chorus)

What! No! You will not join with us?
  Go, seek your wand'ring wits.
This is no place for such as you,
  We'd scare you into fits.

(The Bear rears up and runs this way and that way as they caper around and flash their torches in his face. He grumbles and growls in comical fear, louder and louder. Then, when a chance occurs, he rushes away and disappears.)

(Chorus)

(Now distant thunder is heard. It can be made by rolling a big bowling-ball in a barrel, or by use of a drum. It comes nearer and louder. Flashes of lightning (gunpowder) are seen. The Fire-flies dance away and sing:)

Oh, hear that funny Thunder Storm,
  A-bumbling in the sky;
He thinks he'll stop our dancing now—
  Just wait and see him try.

(The storm grows fearful; a gun fired with heavy blank charges of powder would help the effect. The Fire-flies think it all uproariously funny, and simply dance more and more merrily, laughing and singing the Chorus:)

Twinkle, twinkle, etc.

(The thunder dies away, defeated.)

And thus, you know, we dance away
   The merry summer long,
For we're the Wild-wood Fairies that
   You learn about in song.

(Chorus)

(Now a tall white-blanketed form (Winter) comes slowly into view. The Fire-flies stop dancing and march slowly around, holding the torches up, tremblingly, as they sing to different music—preferably a lullaby, or possibly an adaptation of " Juanita ":)

   Yet is there one we fear,
      Winter so chill.
   Whenever he draws near
      Wild woods are still.

(Winter approaches and throws into air a handful of snow (paper). The Fire-flies continue:)

   Long ere the snowflakes fly
      We should be gone
   Back to our Mother Earth,
      Ere the chill dawn.

   Done is our summer chase.
      Now we retire,
   Dancing lights yielding place
      To the camp-fire.

(They pile their torches—that is, the punks slipped out of the sticks—in the middle at a place prepared with shavings, etc., for a blaze, and they lie down in a ring and sing, by the light of the camp-fire:)

   Low bend we on the Earth,
      Silence to keep;
   Winter has killed our mirth—
      The Fire-flies sleep.

(Repeat last two lines, then again the last, fainter each time, till it dies away.)

Winter stands over and gently sprinkles them with snow. *Curtain* now, if indoors.

If outdoors, Winter might also sprinkle water on the fire till it is out. As he retires from view, the Medicine Man, by clapping, marks the end of the Play, and all rise and run to their seats.

(The games from here to the end of this section are from General Baden-Powell's book.)

LION HUNTING

A lion is represented by one scout, who goes out with tracking irons on his feet, and a pocketful of corn or peas, and six lawn-tennis balls or rag balls. He is allowed half an hour's start, and then the patrol go after him, following his spoor, each armed with one tennis ball with which to shoot him when they find him. The lion may hide or creep about or run, just as he feels inclined, but whenever the ground is hard or very greasy he must drop a few grains of corn every few yards to show the trail.

If the hunters fail to come up to him neither wins the game. When they come near to his lair the lion fires at them with his tennis balls, and the moment a hunter is hit he must fall out dead and cannot throw his tennis ball. If the lion gets hit by a hunter's tennis ball he is wounded, and if he gets wounded three times he is killed.

Tennis balls may only be fired once; they cannot be picked up and fired again in the same fight.

Each scout must collect and hand in his tennis balls after the game. In winter, if there is snow, this game can be played without tracking irons, and using snowballs instead of tennis balls.

PLANT RACE

Start off your scouts, either cycling or on foot, to go in any direction they like, to get a specimen of any ordered plant, say a sprig of yew, a shoot of ilex, a horseshoe mark from a chestnut tree, a briar rose, or something of that kind, whichever you may order, such as will tax their knowledge of plants and will test their memory as to where they noticed one of the kind required, and will also make them quick in getting there and back.

THROWING THE ASSEGAI

Target, a thin sack, lightly stuffed with straw, or a sheet of cardboard, or canvas stretched on a frame.

Assegais to be made of wands, with weighted ends sharpened, or with iron arrow-heads on them.

FLAG RAIDING

(From " Aids to Scouting," 1s.   Gale and Polden)

Two or more patrols on each side.

Each side will form an outpost within a given tract of country to protect three flags (or at night three lanterns two feet above ground), planted not less than 200 yards (100 yards at night) from it.   The protecting outpost will be posted in concealment either all together or spread out in pairs.   It will then send out scouts to discover the enemy's position.   When these have found out where the outpost is, they try and creep round out of sight till they can get to the flags and bring them away to their own line.   One scout may not take away more than one flag.

This is the general position of a patrol on such an outpost:

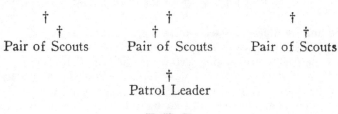

```
    †               †               †
    †               †               †
Pair of Scouts   Pair of Scouts   Pair of Scouts

                    †
              Patrol Leader

                P  P  P
                 Flags
```

Any scout coming within fifty yards of a stronger party will be put out of action if seen by the enemy; if he can creep by without being seen it is all right.

Scouts posted to watch as outposts cannot move from their

ground, but their strength counts as double, and they may send single messengers to their neighbors or to their own scouting party.

An umpire should be with each outpost and with each scouting patrol.

At a given hour operations will cease, and all will assemble at the given spot to hand in their reports. The following points might be awarded:

For each flag or lamp captured and brought in   5 points
For each report or sketch of the position of the
    enemy's outposts.................... up to 5 points
For each report of movement of enemy's scout-
    ing patrols........................   2 points

The side which makes the biggest total wins.

The same game may be played to test the scouts in stepping lightly—the umpire being blindfolded. The practice should preferably be carried out where there are dry twigs lying about, and gravel, etc. The scout may start to stalk the blind enemy at 100 yards' distance, and he must do it fairly fast—say, in one minute and a half—to touch the blind man before he hears him.

STALKING AND REPORTING

The umpire places himself out in the open and sends each scout or pair of scouts away in different directions about half a mile off. When he waves a flag, which is the signal to begin, they all hide, and then proceed to stalk him, creeping up and watching all he does. When he waves the flag again, they rise, come in, and report each in turn all that he did, either by handing in a written report or verbally, as may be ordered. The umpire meantime has kept a lookout in each direction, and, every time he sees a scout, he takes two points off that scout's score. He, on his part, performs small actions, such as sitting down, kneeling up, looking through glasses, using handkerchief, taking hat off for a bit, walking round in a circle a few times, to give scouts something to note and report about him. Scouts are given three points for each act reported correctly. It saves time if the umpire makes out a scoring card beforehand, giving the name of each scout, and a number of columns showing each act of his, and what mark that scout wins, also a column of deducted marks for exposing themselves.

"SPIDER AND FLY"

A bit of country or section of the town about a mile square is selected as the web, and its boundaries described, and an hour fixed at which operations are to cease.

One patrol (or half-patrol) is the "spider," which goes out and selects a place to hide itself.

The other patrol (or half-patrol) goes a quarter of an hour later as the "fly" to look for the "spider." They can spread themselves about as they like, but must tell their leader anything that they discover.

An umpire goes with each party.

If within the given time (say, about two hours) the fly has not discovered the spider, the spider wins. The spiders write down the names of any of the fly patrol that they may see; similarly   .

HOW TO TEACH STALKING

Demonstrate the value of adapting color of clothes to background by sending out one boy about 500 yards to stand against different backgrounds in turn, till he gets one similar in color to his own clothes.

The rest of the patrol to watch and to notice how invisible he becomes when he gets a suitable background. E.g., a boy in a gray suit standing in front of dark bushes, etc., is quite visible— but becomes less so if he stands in front of a gray rock or house; a boy in a dark suit is very visible in a green field, but not when he stands in an open doorway against dark interior shadow.

SCOUT HUNTING

One scout is given time to go out and hide himself, the remainder then start to find him; he wins if he is not found, or if he can get back to the starting-point within a given time without being touched.

RELAY RACE

One patrol pitted against another to see who can get a message sent a long distance in shortest time by means of relays of runners (or cyclists). The patrol is ordered out to send in three successive notes or tokens (such as sprigs of certain plants), from a point, say, two miles distant or more. The leader in taking his patrol out to the spot drops scouts at convenient distances, who will then act as runners from one post to the next and back. If relays are posted in pairs, messages can be passed both ways.

STALKING

Instructor acts as a deer—not hiding, but standing, moving a little now and then if he likes.

Scouts go out to find, and each of his own way tries to get up to him unseen.

Directly the instructor sees a scout, he directs him to stand up as having failed. After a certain time the instructor calls " Time," all stand up at the spot which they have reached, and the nearest wins.

TRACK MEMORY

Make a patrol sit with their feet up, so that other scouts can study them. Give the scouts, say, three minutes to study the boots. Then leaving the scouts in a room or out of sight, let one of the patrol make some footmarks in a good bit of ground. Call up the scouts one by one and let them see the track and say who made it.

SPOT THE THIEF

Get a stranger to make a track unseen by the scouts.   The scouts study his track so as to know it again.

Then put the stranger among eight or ten others and let them all make their tracks for the boys to see, going by in rotation. Each scout then in turn whispers to the umpire which man made the original track—describing him by his number in filing past. The scout who answers correctly wins; if more than one answers correctly, the one who then draws the best diagram, from memory, of the footprint wins.

"SMUGGLERS OVER THE BORDER"

The "border" is a certain line of country about 400 yards long, preferably a road or wide path or bit of sand, on which foot-tracks can easily be seen.   One patrol watches the border with sentries posted along this road, with a reserve posted further inland.   This latter about halfway between the "border" and the "town"; the "town" would be a base marked by a tree, building, or flags, etc., about half a mile distant from the border.   A hostile patrol of smugglers assembles about half a mile on the other side of the border.   They will all cross the border, in any formation they please, either singly or together or scattered, and make for the town, either walking or running, or at scout's pace.   Only one among them is supposed to be smuggling, and he wears tracking irons, so that the sentries walk up and down their beat (they may not run till after the "alarm"), waiting for the tracks of the smuggler.   Directly a sentry sees the track, he gives the alarm signal to the reserve and starts himself to follow up the track as fast as he can.   The reserve thereupon coöperate with them and try to catch the smuggler before he can reach the town.   Once within the boundary of the town he is safe and wins the game.

SHOP WINDOW (OUTDOORS IN TOWN)

Umpire takes a patrol down a street past six shops. Gives them half a minute at each shop, then, after moving them off to some distance, he gives each boy a pencil and card, and tells him to write from memory, or himself takes down, what they noticed in, say, the third and fifth shops. The one who sets down most articles correctly wins. It is useful practice to match one boy against another in heats—the loser competing again, till you arrive at the worst. This gives the worst scouts the most practice.

SIMILAR GAME (INDOORS)

Send each scout in turn into a room for half a minute; when he comes out take down a list of furniture and articles which he notices. The boy who notices most wins.

The simplest way of scoring is to make a list of the articles in the room on your scoring paper with a column for marks for each scout against them, which can then easily be totalled up at foot.

FOLLOW THE TRAIL

Send out a " hare," either walking or cycling, with a pocketful of corn, nutshells, confetti paper, or buttons, etc., and drop a few here and there to give a trail for the patrol to follow.

Or go out with a piece of chalk and draw the patrol sign on walls, gateposts, pavements, lamp-posts, trees, etc., every here and there, and let the patrol hunt you by these marks. Patrols should wipe out all these marks as they pass them for tidiness, and so as not to mislead them for another day's practice.

The other road signs should also be used, such as closing up certain roads as not used, and hiding a letter at some point, giving directions as to the next turn.

SCOUT'S NOSE (INDOORS)

Prepare a number of paper bags, all alike, and put in each a different smelling article, such as chopped onion in one, tan in another, rose leaves, leather, aniseed, violet powder, orange peel, etc. Put these packets in a row a couple of feet apart, and let each competitor walk down the line and have five seconds' sniff at each. At the end he has one minute in which to write down or to state to the umpire the names of the different objects smelled, from memory, in their correct order.

SCOUT MEETS SCOUT

IN TOWN OR COUNTRY

Single scouts, or complete patrols or pairs of scouts, to be taken out about two miles apart, and made to work towards each other, either alongside a road, or by giving each side a landmark to work to, such as a steep hill or big tree, which is directly behind the other party, and will thus insure their coming together. The patrol which first sees the other wins. This is signified by the patrol leader holding up his patrol flag for the umpire to see, and sounding his whistle. A patrol need not keep together, but that patrol wins which first holds out its flag, so it is well for the scouts to be in touch with their patrol leaders by signal, voice, or message.

Scouts may employ any ruse they like, such as climbing into trees, hiding in carts, etc., but they must not dress up in disguise.

This may also be practised at night.

SHOOT OUT

Two patrols compete. Targets: bottles or bricks set up on end to represent the opposing patrol. Both patrols are drawn up in line at about 20 to 25 yards from the targets. At the word "fire," they throw stones at the targets. Directly a target falls, the umpire directs the corresponding man of the other patrol to sit down—killed. The game goes on, if there are plenty of stones, till the whole of one patrol is killed. Or a certain number of stones can be given to each patrol, or a certain time limit, say one minute.

KIM'S GAME

Place about twenty or thirty small articles on a tray, or on the table or floor, such as two or three different kinds of buttons, pencils, corks, rags, nuts, stones, knives, string, photos—anything you can find—and cover them over with a cloth or coat.

Make a list of these, and make a column opposite the list for each boy's replies. Like this:

List.	Jones.	Brown.	Smith.	Atkins.	Green.	Long.
Walnut........						
Button.........						
Black button...						
Red rag........						
Yellow rag....						
Black rag.....						
Knife..........						
Red pencil.....						
Black pencil...						
Cork						
String knot....						
Plain string...						
Blue bead......						

Then uncover the articles for one minute by your watch, or while you count sixty at the rate of "quick march." Then cover them over again.

Take each boy separately and let him whisper to you each of the articles that he can remember, and mark it off on your scoring sheet.

The boy who remembers the greatest number wins the game.

MORGAN'S GAME

(Played by the 21st Dublin Co. Boys' Brigade)

Scouts are ordered to run to a certain hoarding, where an umpire is already posted to time them. They are each allowed to look at this for one minute, and then to run back to headquarters and report to the instructor all that was on the hoarding in the way of advertisements.

SNOW FORT

The snow fort may be built by one patrol according to their own ideas of fortification, with loopholes, etc., for looking out. When finished, it will be attacked by hostile patrols, using snowballs as ammunition. Every scout struck by a snowball is counted dead. The attackers should, as a rule, number at least twice the strength of the defenders.

SIBERIAN MAN HUNT

One scout as fugitive runs away across the snow in any direction he may please until he finds a good hiding-place, and there conceals himself. The remainder, after giving him twenty minutes' start or more, proceed to follow him by his tracks. As they approach his hiding-place, he shoots at them with snowballs, and every one that is struck must fall out dead. The fugitive must be struck three times before he is counted dead.

PART V. THE HONORS

These exploits are intended to distinguish those who are first-class in their department, and those who are so good that they may be considered in the record-making class. They may be called Honors and High Honors, but the Plains Indians speak of their exploits as Coup (pronounced *coo*) and Grand Coup. The Sioux, I am informed, use the French word *coup,* but call them "*Jus-tce-na coo*" and "*Tonka coo,*" the "Little Deed," and the "Big Deed."

Sometimes they are called Feathers and High Feathers. In the Sons-of-Daniel-Boone Camps, founded by Mr. Dan Beard, they are called "Notches" and "Topnotches" on the gun stock. In some groups they are called Stunts and Big Stunts.

No one can count both Honor and High Honor, or repeat their honor in the same department, except for Heroism, Mountain-climbing, and others that are specified as "repeaters," in which each honor is added to that previously worn.

No honors are conferred unless the exploit has been properly witnessed or proven, as though for the Century Bar of the L. A. W. When it is a question of time under one minute, only stop-watches are allowed.

Honors are allowed according to the standard of the year in which the application was made.

An honor, once fairly won, can never be lost for subsequent failure to reach the standard.

Except when otherwise stated, the exploits are meant for all ages.

Any one making honor according to the class above him, may count it a high honor in his own class, unless otherwise provided.

This list is made by the National Council. The exploits are founded on world-wide standards, and with the help of the best experts. The Council will gladly consider any suggestion, but it must be understood that no local group has any power to add to or vary the exploits in any way whatsoever.

CLASS I.   RED HONORS

HEROISM

Honors are allowed for saving a human life at risk of one's own; it is an honor or a high honor, at the discretion of the Council.

A soldier's war medals count for a high honor each.

Courage.   (The measure of courage has not yet been discovered.)

RIDING

To ride a horse 1 mile in 3 minutes, clearing a 4-foot hurdle and an 8-foot water-jump, counts honor; to do it in 2 minutes, clearing a 5-foot hurdle and a 12-foot water-jump, high honor.

Trick-riding.   To pick up one's hat from the ground while at full gallop on a horse of not less than 13 hands, counts honor.

To do it 3 times without failure, from each side, with horse of at least 15 hands, counts high honor.

GENERAL ATHLETICS

(Advisers—J. E. Sullivan, secretary of Amateur Athletic Union; Dr. Luther H. Gulick, director of physical training, New York Public School)

Those under 10 are children; those over 10 and under 14 are boys; those over 14 and under 18 are lads; those over 18 are men.

Girls take the standards according to their ages up to 18, but for athletics are never over that.   No matter what their age, thenceforth they continue in the "lad class," and in filing the claim need only mention their class.

Men over 70 return to the lad class.

The records are given according to Spalding's Almanac, where will be found the names of those who made them, with date and place.

A dash (—) means "not open."

GENERAL ATHLETICS (*Continued*)

	Children *i. e.* under 10		Boys 10 to 14		Lads 14 to 18		Men over 18		Record
	honor	h. h.	honor	h. h.	honor	h. h.	honor	h. h.	
Walking									
50 yards	16 s;	15	14;	13	—	—	—	—	
100 yards	31 s;	29	27;	25	—	—	—	—	
220 yards	70 s;	65	60;	56	—	—	—	—	$36\frac{3}{5}$ s
440 yards	4 m;	$3\frac{1}{2}$	3;	$2\frac{1}{2}$	—	—	—	—	1 m 23 s
880 yards	$6\frac{1}{2}$ m;	6	$5\frac{1}{2}$;	5	—	—	—	—	3 m $2\frac{4}{5}$ s
1 mile	14 m;	13	12;	11	10;	$9\frac{1}{2}$	$8\frac{1}{2}$	$7\frac{3}{4}$	6 m $29\frac{3}{5}$ s
in one hour	—	—	$3\frac{1}{2}$ mi;	4 mi	$4\frac{1}{2}$ mi;	5 mi	$5\frac{1}{2}$ mi	$6\frac{1}{2}$ mi	7 mi; 1318 yds
12 hours	—	—	20 mi;	25 mi	30 mi;	35 mi	40 mi	50 mi	
5 miles	—	—	90 m;	80 m	70 m;	65 m	60 m;	50 m	38 m 58 s
Running									
50 yards	$7\frac{1}{5}$ s;	7	7;	$6\frac{3}{5}$	—	—	—	—	$5\frac{3}{5}$
100 yards	—	—	$14\frac{1}{5}$ s;	$13\frac{3}{5}$	$12\frac{3}{5}$;	$11\frac{4}{5}$	$10\frac{4}{5}$	$10\frac{2}{5}$	$9\frac{3}{5}$
220 yards	—	—	—	—	29;	27	26;	24	$21\frac{95}{100}$
440 yards	—	—	—	—	63;	58	56;	52	47 s
880 yards	—	—	—	—	$2\frac{1}{2}$ m;	$2\frac{1}{8}$	$2\frac{1}{4}$;	$2\frac{1}{8}$	1 m $53\frac{2}{5}$ s
1 mile	—	—	—	—	—	—	$5\frac{1}{4}$ m;	$4\frac{3}{5}$	4 m $15\frac{3}{5}$ s
5 miles	—	—	—	—	—	—	35 m;	30	25 m $23\frac{2}{5}$ s
Running backward									
50 yards	14 s;	13	13;	12	11;	10	9;	8	$7\frac{4}{5}$ s
100 yards	23 s;	22	21;	20	19;	18	17;	16	14 s
Standing high jump without weights	$2\frac{1}{2}$ ft;	$2\frac{3}{4}$	3;	$3\frac{1}{2}$	$3\frac{3}{8}$;	$3\frac{3}{4}$	$4\frac{1}{8}$;	$4\frac{1}{2}$	5 ft $5\frac{1}{4}$ in
Running high jump without weights	3 ft;	$3\frac{1}{4}$	$3\frac{3}{4}$;	$4\frac{1}{4}$	$4\frac{1}{2}$;	$4\frac{3}{4}$	$5\frac{1}{4}$	$5\frac{1}{2}$	6 ft $5\frac{5}{8}$ in
Standing broad jump without weights	5 ft;	$5\frac{1}{2}$	6;	$6\frac{1}{2}$	7;	8;	9;	10	11 ft $3\frac{1}{2}$ in
Running broad jump without weights	12 ft;	13	14;	15	$15\frac{3}{4}$	$16\frac{1}{2}$	$17\frac{1}{2}$;	19	24 ft $7\frac{1}{4}$ in
Hop, step, and jump without weights or run	$13\frac{1}{2}$;	15	16;	19	20;	22	23;	26	30 ft 3 in

GENERAL ATHLETICS (*Continued*)

	Children *i. e.* under 10		Boys 10 to 14		Lads 14 to 18		Men over 18		Record
Hopping on one leg									
50 yards	—	—	13 s;	12	11;	10	9;	8	7½ s
100 yards	—	—	—	—	20 s;	18	17;	16	13⅘ s
Hammer thrown 3½-ft. handle from 7-ft. circle, both hands	—	—	—	—	(12 lb. hammer, 60 ft; 70		(16 lb. hammer) 65, 75		100 ft 5 in
Shot-put 7-ft. circle (12 lb. shot)	—	—	20 ft;	24	28;	30	(16 lb. shot) 36; 40		47 ft
Discus 7-ft. circle (4½ pounds)	—	—	—	—	70 ft;	85	90;	100	128 ft 10½ in
Throw base-ball (regulation)	50 yds; 55		60;	70	75;	95	100;	110	127 yds 2¼ in
Batting baseball	45 yds; 50		55;	65	70;	90	95;	105	118 yds 10 in
Throwing lacrosse ball with stick	70 yds; 80		90;	100	110;	130	130;	150	165 yds; 2 ft 7½ in
Football kick a drop goal	20 yds; 25		30;	35	40;	45	50;	55	63 yds 11 in
Football					may try		High honor: Put two Rugby footballs in middle of Rugby field and kick a right and left goal		
Football Place kick counted to where ball first strikes ground	35 yds; 40		40;	45	45;	50	55;	60	66 yds 2 ft 8 in

GENERAL ATHLETICS (*Continued*)

	Children *i. e.* under 10	Boys 10 to 14	Lads 14 to 18	Men over 18	Record
Running high kick	$5\frac{3}{4}$ ft; 6	$6\frac{1}{4}$; $6\frac{3}{4}$	7; $7\frac{1}{2}$	8; $8\frac{1}{2}$	9 ft 8 in
Climb rope 18 ft.; hands only used	15 s; 14	13; 11	9; 7	6; 5	$3\frac{3}{5}$ secs.
Chin the bar	3 times; 4	6; 8	10; 12	13 15	39 times
Chin bar with one hand			once for honor; once with each hand in succession for high honor	once with each hand honor, twice with each hand high honor	12 times
Hand walk on hands, heels up	5 ft; 10	15; 25	30; 50	75; 100	
Parallel bar 3 successive arm jumps with swings	10 ft; 11	12; 13	14; 15	16; 18	19 ft 9 in
Push up without swing	10 times; 12	15; 18	20; 25	30; 40	58 times
Dumb-bell Put up 5 pounder with one hand to full arm's length above shoulders.	50 times; 100	150 – 200	(10 pounder) 200 – 300	(10 pounder) 400 – 600	8,431 times
Skating					
100 yards	17 s; 16	15; 13	13; 12	$11\frac{1}{5}$; $10\frac{2}{5}$	9 s (with wind)
440 yards	— —	75 s; 70	65; 60	50; 45	35 $\frac{1}{5}$ secs.
880 yards	— —	160 s; 150	145; 140	135; 130	1 m $20\frac{2}{5}$ s
1 mile	— —	4 m; $3\frac{3}{4}$	$3\frac{1}{2}$ $3\frac{1}{5}$	3; $2\frac{5}{6}$	$2\frac{36}{60}$ mins.
5 miles	— —	— —	25 m; 21	19; 17	14 m 24 s
10 miles	— —	— —	55 m; 48	42; 36	31 m $11\frac{1}{5}$ s
15 miles	— —	— —	90 m; 80	70; 60	49 m $17\frac{3}{5}$ s
20 miles	— —	— —	$2\frac{1}{4}$ hr; 2	$1\frac{2}{3}$; $1\frac{1}{3}$	1 hr. 6 m $36\frac{2}{5}$ s
25 miles	— —	— —	3 hr; $2\frac{1}{2}$	$2\frac{1}{2}$; 2	1 hr. 31 m 29 s

GENERAL ATHLETICS (*Continued*)

	Children *i e.* under 10		Boys 10 to 14		Lads 14 to 18		Men over 18		Record
Rowing (single sculls) 1 mile	13 m;	12	11;	10	9;	8	7$\frac{88}{60}$;	6$\frac{88}{60}$	
Paddle (single) 1 mile	15 m;	14	13;	12	12;	11	10;	9	
Swim { 100 yards	any time honor		any time honor		any time honor		any time honor		58 s
200 yards	5 m, h. h.		4 m, h. h.		3$\frac{3}{4}$ m, h. h.		3 m, h. h.		2 m 20 s
1 mile	—	—	—	—	50 m;	45	45;	35	24 m 46$\frac{4}{5}$ s
Medley Race (400 yards) rowing 100 swimming 100 walking 100 running 100	—	—	—	—	6 m;	5	4$\frac{1}{2}$;	4	
Bicycle 1 mile	—	—	—	—	3$\frac{1}{2}$ m;	3	2$\frac{50}{60}$;	2$\frac{80}{60}$	

ATHLETIC SPECIALTIES

LONG DISTANCE ATHLETICS

(Open only to those who are over 21)

```
Run 10 miles, honor 80 m., h. h. 70 m.,  Rec.      52 m.  38⅘ s.
 "  15    "   —  "   2 h.,  "   "  1¾ h.,  Rec. 1 h. 27 "  11⅜ "
 "  20    "   —  "   3  "  "   "  2½  "         "  2 " 13 "   5  "
 "  30    "   —  "   4½ "  "   "  4   "         "  3 " 36 "   3½ "
 "  40    "   —  "   6½ "  "   "  6   "         "  5 " 20½ "  —
 "  50    "   —  "   9  "  "   "  8   "         "  7 " 29 "  47  "
 "  75    "   —  "  16  "  "   " 14   "         " 12 " 20 "  10  "
 " 100    "   —  "  24  "  "   " 21   "         " 17 " 36 "  14  "
```

Walk	10 miles,	honor $1\frac{3}{4}$ h.,	h. h. $1\frac{1}{4}$ h.,	Rec. 1 h. 17 m. $40\frac{3}{4}$ s.
"	15 "	" 3 "	" " $2\frac{3}{4}$ "	" 2 " 14 " 44 "
"	20 "	" 4 "	" " $3\frac{3}{4}$ "	" 3 " 8 " 10 "
"	25 "	" 5 "	" " $4\frac{3}{4}$ "	" 4 " 3 " 35 "
"	30 "	" $7\frac{1}{2}$ "	" " $6\frac{1}{2}$ "	" 5 " 33 " 8 "
"	40 "	" 10 "	" " 9 "	" 7 " 25 " 41 "
"	50 "	" 13 "	" " 12 "	" 9 " 29 " 22 "
"	75 "	" 18 "	" " $16\frac{1}{2}$ "	" 15 " 0 " 15 "
"	100 "	" 30 "	" " 25 "	" 21 " 0 " 42 "
Skate	50 miles,	honor 5 h.,	h. h. 4 h.,	Rec. 3 h., 15 m. $59\frac{2}{5}$ s.
"	75 "	" $7\frac{1}{2}$ "	" " 6 "	" 5 " 19 " $16\frac{4}{5}$ "
"	100 "	" 12 "	" " 10 "	" 7 " 11 " $38\frac{1}{5}$ "
Swim	5 miles,	honor 4 h.,	h. h. $3\frac{1}{2}$ h.,	Rec. 2 h. 58 m. $0\frac{1}{2}$ s.
"	10 "	" in any time		
"	15 "	high honor in any time		

Bicycle 100 miles in 24 hrs., honor
" 200 " in 24 hrs., high honor
(Acc. to L. A. W. rules)

Weight-throwing. Throw the 56-lb. weight from a 7-ft. circle: h. 22 ft.; h. h. 28 ft.; Rec. 38 ft. 7⅜ in.

Dumb-bell. Pushing up one 50-lb. dumb-bell with one hand to full arm length above the shoulder: 15 times for honor; 30 times, high honor; Rec. 94 times.

Ditto with 100-lb. dumb-bell: 5 times, honor; 10 times, high honor; Rec. 20 times.

Ditto with two 100-lb. dumb-bells once; one in each hand, same time, high honor.

To turn a wheel, honor.

Handspring. To throw a tumbler or 4-legged handspring, honor; to throw a clean handspring, high honor.

Back handspring. A clean back handspring, high honor.

WATER-SPORTS AND TRAVEL

(For swimming, rowing, etc., see classified athletics on a previous page)

Bathing. An honor for having bathed out of doors in water of natural temperature anywhere north of N. Lat. 30, or south of S. Lat. 30 for 300 days in the year; a high honor for 365 days.

Sailing. To have sailed any two-man craft for 30 successive days, 12 hours a day at the wheel,—the other man not a professional sailor,—honor.

Sixty days of the same in salt water, high honor.

Log-riding. Tread a sawlog 100 yards in any time, without going overboard, for honor; do it 100 yards and back in 30 minutes, for high honor.

Canoeman. An honor is allowed to those who can paddle (single) a canoe on dead water, make their paddling honor (see p. 178), spill the canoe and get into her again, and bale her alone.

A high honor, when they make their paddling honor, spill, right, and bale the canoe alone, three times in succession, and have run a rapid that falls 6 feet in 200 yards.

Canoe-camper. To have made a continuous canoe trip of 500 miles, sleeping out every night, honor; 1,000 miles of the same, high honor.

Saddle-camper. To have made a continuous saddle trip of 500 miles, sleeping out every night, honor; 1,000 miles, high honor.

Camper. An honor, for passing 30 successive nights out of doors, never once sleeping under shingles, but in tent, teepee, or bivouac, every night. A high honor, for 60 nights of the same.

Lone-tramper. An honor, for travelling alone, on foot, 100 miles, carrying one's outfit, sleeping out every night; a high honor, for 200 miles.

Gang-tramper. An honor, for travelling 150 miles on foot with a party, carrying one's own outfit, sleeping out every night; a high honor, for 250 miles.

Ski-man. To have travelled 6 miles in an hour, 40 miles in one day, covered 40 feet in a jump, and travelled 500 miles all told, counts an honor.

To have travelled 7 miles in an hour, 50 miles in one day, made a 50-foot jump, and travelled 1,000 miles all told, counts a high honor.

Arctic Traveller. An honor, for entering the Arctic Circle by sea; a high honor, by land.

Tropic Traveller. An honor, for crossing the Equator by sea or rail; a high honor, on foot.

Motoring. To have covered 1,000 miles within 30 days, acting as your own chauffeur and mechanic, honor. To have covered 1,000 miles in 4 days, 100 miles in 2 hours, acting as your own chauffeur and mechanic, high honor.

(In both cases garage privileges allowed.)

MOUNTAIN-CLIMBING (All Afoot)

(Not open to boys, *i.e.*, those under 14)

By Sir Martin Conway, ex-President of the Alpine Club

The exploits in this class are repeaters.

The first one to climb a standard peak gets double honors; one for *climb,* one for *first climb.*

For lads (*i.e.*, over 14 and under 18)

HONOR

In Great Britain—Ben Macdhuie; Ben Nevis; Ben Lomond; Ben Cruachan; Snowdon; Scarfell.
In Europe—Vesuvius, Breithorn.
In North America—Mt. Washington; Electric Peak, Wyo.

HIGH HONOR

In Europe—Mt. Blanc; Monte Viso; Etna; Monte Rosa.
In North America—Pike's Peak; Shasta; Adams.
In Asia—Fujiyama; Tabor.
Add to this all the honor list of next.

For men (*i.e.*, all over 18)

HONOR

In Europe—Mont Blanc, Monte Rosa, Monte Viso, Ecrins, Grand Paradis, Jungfrau, Finsteraarhorn, Wetterhorn, Bernina, Ortler, Gross Glockner, Matterhorn from Zermatt.
In North America—St. Helen's; Adams; Shasta; Hood; Rainier; Mt. Shaughnessy; Mt. Stephen; Popocatepetl; Orizaba.

In Europe—Meije, Aig. du Grépon, Aig. du Géant, Aig. du Drü, Matterhorn (by Italian or Stockje ridges), Dent Blanche, Mischabelhörner from Seas, Schreckhorn, Monte di Scerscen, Fünffinger Sp., Kleine Zinne.

In North America—Mt. Sir Donald, Mt. Logan, Mt. Assiniboine, Mt. Fairweather, Mt. St. Elias, Grand Teton, Mt. McKinley. Any peak in Alaska over 13,000 feet high.

In South America—Chimborazo, Cotopaxi, Illimani, Aconcagua.

In Asia—Any peak over 19,000 feet high.

In Africa—Any peak over 15,000 feet high.

TARGET-SHOOTING

(Open to men only)

Everything that can be said in favor of firearms for use in general sport applies to the rifle only (and its understudy the revolver). The scatter-gun has no official existence for us. It is ruination to the marksman's power and should be abolished. A rifle range is a desirable adjunct to all grown-up camps. Honors awarded according to the army standards.

Revolver-shot. Target 4 x 4 feet. Bull's eye 8 inches (counts 4 points). Inner ring 2 feet (3 points). Outer, the rest of target (2 points).

Distance, 30 yards.

Ninety-six shots divided in any number up to six days, one hand, standing:

250 points count honor; 300, high honor.

Half with left hand only; half with right only:

230 points, honor; 260, high honor.

Rifleman. To be a *marksman* of the highest rank but one, according to militia standards, an honor; to be an *expert rifleman* of the highest rank, a high honor.

EYESIGHT

To spot the Rabbit three times out of five at 60 yards, also to distinguish and map out correctly six Pleiades and see clearly the " Pappoose (Alcor) on the Squaw's (Mizar) back," counts an honor; to spot the Rabbit three times out of five at 70 yards and seven Pleiades and the Pappoose, counts a far-sight high honor. (Those who habitually wear glasses may use them in this test.) (See " Far-sight," among the games, p. 149.)

To make a 75 score in ten tries in the game of Quick-sight, with ten counters, counts honor; a 95 score counts a high honor. (See " Quick-sight," among the games, p. 148.)

BIG-GAME HUNTING

(By permission of the Camp-fire Club of America)

Inasmuch as Hunting Big Game must be recognized in our list of national outdoor sports, it should be elevated to a higher plane by the adoption of these rules, because they tend to give the utmost prominence to the many admirable features of the chase, and at the same time reduce the total sum of destruction.

To have gone alone into the haunts of big game, that is to say, without professional guide, and by fair hunting, unaided by traps or poison, or dogs (except where marked " d "), have killed and saved for good purposes, *in absolute accordance with the game laws,* any of the following kinds of game (or others of a corresponding character), counts honors as below:

Each species counts one honor; that is, one Tiger would count one honor, ten Tigers would not count any more, and when he gets his Tiger, his Moose, etc., the sportsman is supposed to stop so far as that species is concerned.

The presence of a professional hunter reduces a high honor to an honor, and if he took any part in the actual killing it does not count at all. A native gun-bearer is not necessarily a professional guide.

HONOR

Black-bear   (d)   Water-buck
Puma   (d)   Deer
Gray-wolf   (d)   Moose, Wapiti, etc.
Wild Boar, otherwise than Tiger (from elephant-back or
    with spear (d)   Machan)
Caribou   14-foot Crocodile or Alligator

HIGH HONOR

Elephant   Hippopotamus
Lion   Moose (by stalking)
Tiger (without help of ele- Mountain Goat
    phants)   Mountain Sheep, adult ram
Jaguar   Chamois
Leopard   Himalayan Tahr, adult male
Puma   Gray-wolf
Rhinoceros   Grizzly-bear
Indian Bison   Spectacled Bear
African Buffalo   Wild Boar, with spear, etc.
Gorilla   Sword-fish, 15 feet long, from
Okapi   small boat

CLASS II. WHITE HONORS

CAMPERCRAFT AND SCOUTING

Bee-line. Come to camp through strange woods from a point one mile off and return in 30 minutes, for honor; in 20 for high honor.

Match-fire. Light 15 camp-fires in succession with 15 matches, all in different places, all with stuff found in the woods by himself, one at least to be on a wet day, for honor; if all 15 are done on wet days, or if he does 30, of which two are on wet days, it counts high honor.

Flint and Steel Fire. To light 15 camp-fires in succession with wildwood tinder, one at least on a wet day, and none to take over a minute from striking the flint, to having the blazes, honor; if all 15 are done on one day, or if he does 30 fires in unbroken succession, two at least on wet days, and in no case more than half a minute from strike to blaze, high honor.

Rubbing-stick Fire. Light a fire with fire-drill or rubbing sticks, with material of one's own gathering, counts honor; to do it in one minute counts high honor.

Axeman. To chop down three 6-inch trees in succession in 60 seconds each, throwing them to drive each a given stake, honor; in 45 seconds each, high honor.

Knots. To make 30 different standard knots in a rope, for honor; 50 for high honor.

Lasso. To catch 10 horses or cattle in corral, with 10 throws of the lasso, counts honor; to catch 10 on the range in 10 throws counts a high honor.

Lasso. To catch a horse or beef by each of his four feet in four successive throws, high honor.

Lasso. To catch, throw, and " hog-tie " a beef or horse in 2½ minutes for honor, in 1½ minutes for high honor. The record is said to be 40 seconds.

Diamond Hitch. Pack a horse with not less than 100 pounds of stuff, with diamond hitch, to hold during 8 hours of travel, honor. Ten days in succession, a high honor.

Size-guessing. To guess one inch, one foot, one yard, one rod, one acre, 100 yards, 200 yards, one-quarter mile, one-half mile, and a mile, within 20 per cent. of average error, for honor; 10 per cent. for high honor.

Height and Weight Guessing. To guess the height of 10 trees or other high things, and the weight of 10 stones or other things ranging from one ounce to 100 pounds, within 10 per cent. of average error, for honor; 5 per cent. for high honor.

Gauging-farness. To measure the height of 10 trees without climbing, or 10 distances across a river, etc., without crossing, within 10 per cent. of average error, for honor; 5 per cent. for high honor. Tools: an axe and a pocket rule only.

Star-gazing. Know and name 15 star groups, for honor; know 20 star groups and tell the names and something about at least one star in each, for high honor.

Latitude. Take the latitude from the stars at night with a cartwheel, or some home-made instrument, 10 times from different points, within one degree of average error, for honor; one-half degree for high honor.

Traveller. An honor for being able to take correct latitude, longitude, and local time. A high honor for having passed the Royal Geographical Society's examination of " expert traveller."

Red Cross. A high honor for having passed the Red Cross examination of first aid to the wounded.

Boat-builder. Build a boat that will carry two men and that can be paddled, rowed, or sailed by them 6 miles an hour, honor; 7 miles an hour, high honor.

Birch Canoe. To have made a birch canoe that has travelled, with at least one man aboard, 100 miles or more in safety, high honor.

In Sign-talking, to know and use correctly 50 signs, for honor; 100 signs, high honor.

Wig-wag Signalling. To know the semaphore code and signal, as well as receive a message a quarter mile off, at the rate of 10 words a minute, for honor.

The same, at a mile, 24 words a minute, for high honor.

Trailing. Know and clearly discriminate the tracks of 25

of our common wild quadrupeds, also trail one for a mile and
secure it, without aid of snow, honor. Similarly discriminate 50
tracks, and follow 3 tracks a mile as before, but for 3 different
animals, high honor.

ARCHERY

REVISED BY WILL H. THOMPSON, OF SEATTLE, WASH.

Make a total score of 300 with 60 shots (in one or two meets),
4-foot target at 40 yards (or 3-foot target at 30 yards), for
honor; make 400 for high honor.

Shoot so fast and far as to have 6 arrows in the air at once,
for honor; 7, for high honor. (According to Catlin, the record
is 8.)

For children (under 10), to send an arrow 90 yards, honor;
115 yards, high honor. For boys (10 to 14), to send an arrow
125 yards, honor; 150, high honor. For lads (14 to 18), to
send an arrow 175 yards, honor; 200, high honor. For men
(over 18), to send an arrow 250 yards, honor; 275, high honor.

To hit the Burlap Deer in the heart, first shot:

For Boys at 45 yards, honor; 55 yards, high honor
  " Lads " 60   "   " 70 "   "   "
  " Men " 75   "   " 85 "   "   "

(The heart is 9 inches across)

To cover a mile:

Children in 19 shots for honor; 15 shots for high honor
Boys   " 14 "   "   " 11 "   "   "   "
Lads   " 10 "   "   " 9 "   "   "   "
Men   " 8   "   "   " 7 "   "   "   "

LONG RANGE, CLOUT, OR FLIGHT SHOOTING

Lads. Three-foot target at 130 yards, if possible on a steep hillside.

In the target is a bull's eye, and counts........ 9
Within 3 feet of outside of target   "   7
"   6 "   "   "   "   "   "   5
"   9 "   "   "   "   "   "   3
"   12 "   "   "   "   "   "   1

Honor is for 300 at 60 consecutive shots.
High honor is for 400 at 60 consecutive shots.
(In one or two meets)

Men. Four-foot target at 180 yards, if possible on a steep hillside.

In the target is a bull's eye, and counts........ 9
Within 6 feet of outside of target   "   7
"   12 "   "   "   "   "   "   5
"   18 "   "   "   "   "   "   3
"   24 "   "   "   "   "   "   1

Honor for 300 at 60 consecutive shots.
High honor for 400 at 60 consecutive shots.
(In one or two meets)

FISHING

By Dr. Henry van Dyke, Author of "Little Rivers,"
"Fisherman's Luck," etc.

(Boys are those under 14; lads, 14 to 18; men, over 18)

Tackle-making. Boys: To make a 6-foot leader of clean gut, with smooth knots to stand a strain of 5 lbs., honor. To tie 6 different flies, of regular patterns, on number 8-12 hooks, and take trout with each of them, by daylight casting, in clear water, high honor.

Lads: To make a bait rod of 3 joints, straight and sound, 14 oz. or less in weight, 10 feet or less in length, to stand a strain of 1½ lbs. at the tip, 13 lbs. at the grip, honor. To make a jointed fly-rod 8-10 feet long, 4-6 ozs. in weight, capable of casting a fly 60 feet, high honor.

Fly-fishing. Boys and lads: To take with the fly, unassisted, a 3-lb. trout or black bass, on a rod not more than 5 oz. in weight, honor. To take a 5-lb. trout or black bass or a 4-lb. landlocked salmon under the same conditions, high honor.

Men: To hook and land with the fly, unassisted, without net or gaff, a trout or landlocked salmon over 4 lbs., or a salmon over 12 lbs., honor. To take, under the same conditions, a salmon over 25 lbs., high honor.

General Fishing. Boys, lads, and men: To take on a rod, without assistance in hooking, playing, or landing, a trout, black bass, pike, muscallonge, grayling, salmon, bluefish, weakfish, striped bass, kingfish, sheepshead, or other game fish, whose weight in pounds equals or exceeds that of the rod in ounces, honor.

To take under the same conditions, a game fish that is double in pounds the ounces of the rod, high honor.

Indoor Fly-casting. Boys: To cast a fly with a rod of 5 oz. or less, not over 10 feet long, 40 feet, honor; 55 feet, high honor.

Lads: 65 feet, honor; 80 feet, high honor.

Men: 80 feet, honor; 95 feet, high honor.

" Every fish caught and kept, but not used, is a rotten spot in the angler's record " (H. v. D.).

BAIT-CASTING

REVISED BY LOU S. DARLING, OF NEW YORK
(Author of " Tournament Casting and the Proper Equipment ")

With ¼-oz. dummy frog, 5-foot rod, indoors, overhead casting, tournament style :

Child class,	40	feet for honor;	50	feet for high honor				
Boy "	60	" "	"	70	"	"	"	"
Lad "	80	" "	"	90	"	"	"	"
Man "	100	" "	"	120	"	"	"	"

If out of doors add 10 per cent. to each of the distances, if cast is made with the wind.

If a wooden plug is used instead of the dummy-frog, add 30 per cent. to each distance.

CLASS III. BLUE HONORS

NATURE STUDY—VERTEBRATES

REVISED BY FRANK M. CHAPMAN, OF THE AMERICAN MUSEUM OF NATURAL HISTORY, NEW YORK CITY

Know and name correctly 25 native wild quadrupeds, for honor; know and name correctly 50, and tell something about each, for high honor.

Know and draw unmistakable pictures of 25 tracks of our four-foot animals, for honor; of 50 for high honor.

Know and name correctly 100 of our native birds as seen mounted in a museum, the female and young to count separately, when they are wholly different from the male. This counts honor; 200 birds for high honor.

Know and name correctly 50 wild birds in the field; this counts honor; 100, high honor.

Recognize 50 wild birds by note, for honor; 100 for high honor.

Know and name 10 turtles for honor; 20 for high honor, with something interesting about each.

Know and name 10 different snakes, telling which are poisonous, for honor; 20 snakes for high honor.

Know and name correctly 10 Batrachians for honor; 20 for high honor.

Know and name 25 fish for honor; 50 fish for high honor.

NATURE STUDY—LOWER FORMS OF LIFE

REVISED BY JOHN BURROUGHS

Know and name 25 native land and fresh-water shells, for honor; 50 for high honor.

Know and name 25 moths, for honor; 50 for high honor.

Know and name 25 butterflies, for honor; 50 for high honor.

Know and name 50 other insects, for honor; 100 for high honor.

Know and name correctly, *i.e.*, with the accepted English names, according to any standard authority, 25 trees, and tell something interesting about them, counts honor; 50 for high honor.

Know and name correctly 50 of our wild flowers, for honor; 100 for high honor.

Know and name correctly 25 of our wild ferns, for honor; 50 for high honor.

Know and name correctly 25 of our native mosses, for honor; 50 for high honor.

Know and name 50 common toadstools or mushrooms, for honor; 100 for high honor.

GEOLOGY, ETC.

REVISED BY PROFESSOR CHARLES D. WALCOTT, SECRETARY SMITHSONIAN INSTITUTION

Paleontology. Know and name, referring to their proper strata, 50 native fossils, for honor; 100 for high honor.

Mineralogy. Know and name 50 minerals, for honor; 100 for high honor.

Geology. Know and name and describe the 14 great divisions of the earth's crust, according to Geikie, also define watershed, delta, drift, fault, glacier, terrace, stratum, dip, and identify 10 different kinds of rock, for honor. In addition to the first, define sediment metamorphic, anticlinal, synclinal, moraine, coal, metal, mineral, petroleum, and identify in all 20 kinds of rock, for high honor.

PHOTOGRAPHY

Revised by A. Radclyffe Dugmore, of " Country Life in America," New York

Make a good recognizable photograph of any wild bird larger than a robin, while on its nest, for honor. With image 3 inches long for high honor.

Make a good photograph of a Ruffed Grouse drumming, a Prairie-chicken dancing, a Woodcock or a Wild Turkey strutting, for high honor.

Make a good recognizable photograph of a wild animal in the air, for honor, or high honor, according to merit.

Ditto for a fish.

Get a good photograph of any large wild animal in its native surroundings, *and not looking at you,* for honor or high honor, according to merit.

(As these are tests of Woodcraft, menagerie animals do not count.)

Made in United States
Orlando, FL
03 December 2024

54871448R00125